Report Formatting

T. James Crawford
Professor of Business
Indiana University

Jerry W. Robinson
Senior Editor
South-Western Publishing Co.

Lawrence W. Erickson
Formerly Assistant Dean
Graduate School of Education
University of California, Los Angeles

Arnola C. Ownby
Professor of Office Administration
and Business Education
Southwest Missouri State University,
Springfield

Lee R. Beaumont
Professor of Business, Emeritus
Indiana University of Pennsylvania

Computer adaptation by Jerry W. Robinson and
National Evaluation Systems, Inc.

Published by

Z12U   **SOUTH-WESTERN PUBLISHING CO.**

CINCINNATI   WEST CHICAGO, IL   DALLAS   PELHAM MANOR, NY   LIVERMORE, CA

CONTENTS

CONTENTS

CONTENT OF REPORT FORMATTING DISKS

Overview

The Microcomputer Keyboarding/Formatting Applications series consists of three instructional programs:

- Letter Formatting
- Report Formatting
- Table Formatting

This User's Guide and the accompanying two microcomputer disks are for the Report Formatting Program. The User's Guide will provide you with all the instructions you need to go through the program and to operate the microcomputer.

The Report Formatting program has the following learning goals:

(1) Develop skill in formatting unbound, leftbound, and topbound reports.
(2) Improve skills in operating typewriting and word processing equipment.
(3) Improve keyboarding skills.

The program is designed to be used by high school students, post-secondary students, and individuals interested in self-instruction in report formatting and keyboarding. Some previous instruction in typing or keyboarding is recommended. No prior experience with a computer is necessary. This Report Formatting program provides an excellent supplement to *College Keyboarding/Typewriting*, 11th ed., Complete and Intensive Courses, published by South-Western Publishing Co. However, these texts are not necessary; this guide contains all the instructional material and report assignments necessary to complete the program.

Program Organization

This guide and the accompanying software are organized into three instructional modules:

Module A: Unbound Reports
Module B: Leftbound Reports
Module C: Topbound Reports

Each module begins with a Formatting Guides section. The Formatting Guides provide the rules for preparing the reports in the module. You will find a sample of a correctly formatted report in this section. You should read this section before preparing any reports, and you should refer back to it whenever you have questions.

One or more of the following three parts are also included in each module.

(1) *Computer-formatted exercises.* The computer-formatted exercises guide you through keying a set of reports on the microcomputer. The computer will prompt you to key each part of the report, and it will format the report automatically.

(2) *Typewriter simulation.* The typewriter simulation lets you use the computer like a typewriter. You will use the typewriter simulation to key a set of reports. When keying these reports, you will be responsible for all formatting decisions.

(3) *Word processor simulation.* The word processor simulation lets you use the computer like a word processor. As with the typewriter simulation, you will make your own formatting decisions when preparing a set of reports.

Modules A and B contain all three parts. Module C contains two parts: the typewriter simulation and the word processor simulation. There are two Report Formatting disks for this program. Disk 1 is to be used with Module A (Unbound Reports). Disk 2 is to be used with Modules B and C (Leftbound and Topbound Reports). You will be given instructions in this Guide when you should use the disks.

This User's Guide will guide you through the preparation of reports in a step-by-step manner. It contains the copy of the reports that you will key using the computer-formatted exercises, typewriter simulation, and word processor simulation. You may also prepare your own reports using the typewriter and word processor simulations.

Equipment and Materials

You will need the following equipment to use the Report Formatting program.

Apple Version
- Apple IIe microcomputer with Apple IIe 80-Column Text Card
- monochromatic monitor
- one or two disk drives
- 10-pitch parallel or serial printer

TRS-80 Version
- TRS-80 Model III or Model 4 microcomputer
- one or two disk drives
- 10-pitch parallel printer

IBM Version
- IBM PC microcomputer
- monochromatic or RGB color monitor
- one or two disk drives
- 10-pitch parallel printer

In order for your reports to print with the correct top and bottom margins, the paper must be set correctly. If necessary, adjust the paper feeder so that the printer head is just below the perforation on the top line of the paper.

This program calls for underlining in some reports. In order for underlining to work correctly, the printer must be able to backspace. If your printer does not backspace, it is recommended that you omit the underlines.

"Powering Up" the Microcomputer

To "power up" the microcomputer with a Report Formatting disk, follow these directions:

Apple or IBM Version
(1) Insert the disk into the drive, with the label facing up and the oval-cutout end first. (If you have two drives, use Drive #1 on the Apple microcomputer. On the IBM microcomputer, use Drive A, the left drive.)
(2) Close the disk drive door.
(3) Switch the microcomputer and the monitor to "on."

TRS-80 Version
(1) Switch the microcomputer to "on."
(2) When the red light on the disk drive goes off, insert the disk into the drive (the bottom drive on a two-drive microcomputer) with the label facing up and the oval-cutout end first.
(3) Close the disk drive door.
(4) Press the orange RESET key on the right side of the keyboard.
(5) When the TRS-DOS Model III copyright appears on the screen, press RESET again.

"Powering Down" the Microcomputer

To "power down" the microcomputer, follow these steps:

Apple or IBM Version
(1) Exit to the title screen (strike ESC).
(2) Open the disk drive door(s) and remove the disk(s).
(3) Switch the microcomputer and the monitor to "off."

TRS-80 Version
(1) Exit to the title screen (strike CLEAR).
(2) Open the disk drive door(s) and remove the disk(s).
(3) Switch the microcomputer to "off."

Using a Data Disk

All assignments can be keyed and a printed copy can be generated without using a data disk. However, it is a good idea to use a data disk so that you can save documents and access them at a later time. You must use a data disk for the following two situations:

(1) If you want to start a report in one session and finish or edit it in another.
(2) If you are sharing printers and you will be printing reports at another computer.

Instructions for creating a data disk are provided in Appendix A of this guide.

Inserting the data disk. To insert the data disk, follow these instructions:

(1) If the microcomputer you are using has two disk drives, insert the data disk in the second drive. The disk must be inserted with the label facing up and the cutout end first.
(2) If the microcomputer you are using has only one disk drive, remove the Report Formatting disk and insert the data disk (label facing up and cutout end first) into the drive.

NOTE: Insert your data disk only when instructions to do so appear on the microcomputer screen.

NEVER open a disk drive door when the red light is on.

Using the Report Formatting Disks

Signing on. Each time you power up your microcomputer, you will proceed through a sequence of introductory screens. Use the following procedures whenever you begin a session at the microcomputer:

(1) Follow the instructions on page 2 to power up the computer. The title screen will appear.
(2) Follow the instructions on the screen for advancing to the screen titled "Sign-On."

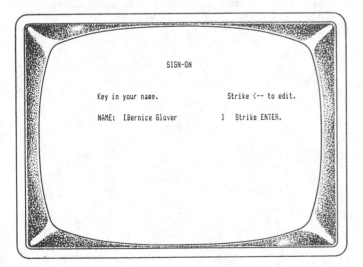

(3) Enter your name as you want it to appear on all printed assignments. Release keys quickly to prevent repeating. If you make a mistake, use the ← key to erase. Once you have entered your name, the following will appear.

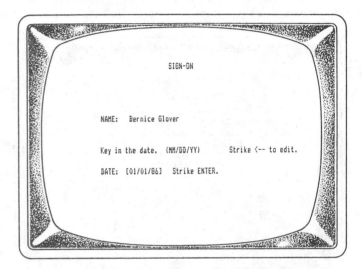

(4) Enter the date in the format of month (two digits), day (two digits), and year (two digits). Your name and this date will appear on a separate document identification page after each report is printed.

(5) Once you complete the Sign-On screen, follow the instructions at the bottom of the screen to proceed to the Main Menu. This menu allows you to choose where to go in the program. Depending on the type of assignments you are working on, you will choose computer-formatted exercises, typewriter simulation, or word processor simulation.

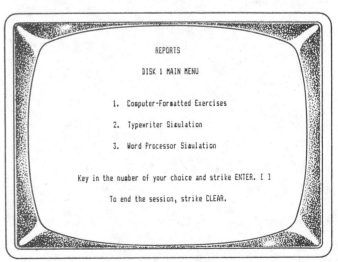

Document management functions. This microcomputer system will enable you to perform many different functions with the documents you create. For each type of simulation, there will be a Functions Menu that lets you select these different functions.

For instance, when you work on the typewriter simulation, you will see a Functions Menu that looks like this:

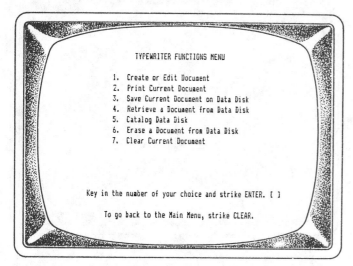

```
        TYPEWRITER FUNCTIONS MENU

    1.  Create or Edit Document
    2.  Print Current Document
    3.  Save Current Document on Data Disk
    4.  Retrieve a Document from Data Disk
    5.  Catalog Data Disk
    6.  Erase a Document from Data Disk
    7.  Clear Current Document




    Key in the number of your choice and strike ENTER. [ ]

    To go back to the Main Menu, strike CLEAR.
```

This menu lists seven functions that you could perform:

(1) *Create or Edit Document.* Select this option whenever you want to create, view, or edit a document. If you are creating a new document, you will receive a screen for entering text. If you are viewing or editing a document you have already created, the text of the document will appear on the screen after you select this option.
NOTE: You cannot edit documents you create in the computer-formatted exercises. However, there is an option that allows you to view the documents.

(2) *Print Current Document.* This function allows you to print a document that you have created, edited, or retrieved (see Function 4). Follow the directions on the screen to print a document.

(3) *Save Current Document on Data Disk.* This option allows you to save onto a data disk a document that you have created or edited. You give each document that you save a name. You are given directions on the screen for saving a document.

If you revise a document after saving it, it is not necessary to erase the document before saving it again. The revised document automatically replaces the old version, as long as you use the same name to save it.

(4) *Retrieve a Document from Data Disk.* Select this function to retrieve a document that you have created. After retrieving a document, you can view, edit, or print it. Follow the directions on the screen for retrieving a document.

(5) *Catalog Data Disk.* When you choose this function, the screen lists the names of all the documents that have been saved on the data disk. Choose this option if you forget the name of a document or if you want to check whether a document has been saved.

(6) *Erase a Document from Data Disk.* This option allows you to erase a saved document from the data disk. Select this option if you no longer want to save a document on the data disk. If your data disk becomes full, you will receive instructions to erase one or more documents to make room for new documents.

(7) *Clear Current Document (Typewriter and Word Processor Simulations only).* If you have created or retrieved a document, you must clear the document from the computer's memory before you can create or retrieve another document. Choose this option to clear the current document.

MODULE A:
UNBOUND REPORTS

UNBOUND REPORTS:
Formatting Guides

Parts of a Report

Reports, as commonly used in business, are written accounts of activities or presentations of information on specified topics. They differ from letter messages in purpose and in format. All reports contain at least the first two of the following parts; longer formal reports typically include all of them.

1. main heading (title)
2. body (text)
3. side headings
4. paragraph headings
5. reference citations
6. reference list
   (or bibliography)
7. cover (title) page

In addition to these standard parts, long reports may include a contents page, a list of figures or tables (or both), an index, and appendices.

This introduction to report formatting is limited to the standard parts listed above.

Unbound Format

Reports may be bound into covers (along the left or the top edge), or they may be left unbound. The pages of multiple-page unbound reports are usually fastened together across the upper left-hand corner with paper clips, staples, or some other fastening device. Unlike bound reports, however, no extra space is left in the margin for fastening the pages together.

Standard margins. In unbound report format, as shown on the facing page, 1-inch (1″) *side margins* are used for all pages (10 pica spaces, 12 elite spaces). On computers, however, final margin width (or line length) is often set when the document is ready for print-out on a printer attached to the computer.

A *top margin* of about 2 inches is customarily used for the first page of unbound reports. This means that the title or main heading appears on line 12. (In school settings where the same report may be typed or printed out on both 10-pitch and 12-pitch machines or printers, a top margin of 1½ inches (line 10) for 10-pitch machines may be used so that all students have similar end-of-page decisions to make.) For the unbound reports in this book, it is recommended that you begin on *line 10.*

A *top margin* of about 1 inch is used for the second page and subsequent pages of unbound reports—the page number placed on line 6 and the text continuing on line 8.

A *bottom margin* of at least 1 inch is recommended for all pages.

Because all reports in this book are to be prepared in double-space mode, vertical placement and spacing guides are given in even numbers: 2, 4, 6, 8, 10, 12 or equivalent line numbers.

Standard Placement and Spacing of Report Parts

Main heading. The main heading or title is centered about 2 inches below the top edge of the page (line 10 for 10-pitch machines or line 12 for 12-pitch machines). The heading is shown in ALL-CAP letters. If two lines are required for the heading, the lines are usually double-spaced (DS) but single-spacing (SS) is acceptable.

Body. The body or text of the report begins a quadruple space (QS) below the main heading, thus leaving 3 blank line spaces between heading and body. The paragraphs of the body are typically double-spaced; but some companies prefer single spacing, particularly for long reports. Double spacing is used between paragraphs regardless of whether the paragraphs are single-spaced or double-spaced.

Side headings. A side heading indicates a subdivision of the main topic. Side headings are placed at the left margin with a double space left above them and a double space left below them. Side headings are shown in capital-and-lowercase letters (first and important words capitalized) and are underlined for emphasis.

Paragraph headings. A paragraph heading indicates a subdivision of the topic of the side heading which precedes it. Paragraph headings are indented five spaces from the left margin, are shown with only the first and proper names capped, end with a period, and are underlined. The copy which follows them begins on the same line two spaces after the period.

Page numbers. The first page of a report is not numbered. On the second page and subsequent pages, the page number is placed at the right margin on line 6. The body continues a double space below beginning on line 8.

Reference citations. References to sources consulted in preparing a report or quoted in the body of a report are cited within the text. The citation includes the name(s) of the author(s), the date of the referenced publication, and the page number(s) of the material cited. (See model, page 7.)

DS

Side headings. Side headings show the major subdivisions of the main heading or topic. They announce the main ideas of the report message. They appear in capital-and-lowercase letters at the left margin with a blank line space left above and below them. Because of their importance, they are underlined. Placing them on separate lines and underlining them give them emphasis.

DS

Paragraph headings. Paragraph headings indicate further subdivisions of the main ideas represented by the side headings. They are indented as part of the first line of the paragraph, are underlined, and end with a period. Only the first word and proper names are capitalized in paragraph headings.

DS

Reference List

DS

The list of references used in compiling the report is the last page of most reports, except for long reports that have appendices or an index. The reference list, sometimes called a bibliography, together with author/date/page citations within the body of the report are called the report's documentation.

All references cited within the report must appear in the reference list (Seybold and Young, 1982, 420). Other references used for verifying information may also be included. The reference list should not be "padded." On the other hand, it should be sufficient to lend credibility to the content of the report.

Start heading or title on line 10.

Line 10

THREE MAJOR PARTS OF SHORT REPORTS

Leave 3 blank line spaces.

DS

Short reports consist of three major parts: a title page, the body or text, and a reference list or bibliography. Each of these parts is briefly described here in order of occurrence in a report.

DS

Title Page

DS

The title page or cover page gives the title of the report; the name of the writer; the name of the school, business, or organization for which the report was prepared; and the date on which the report was completed (House and Sigler, 1981, 181).

The title page answers the important questions what, who, where, and when.

DS

Body or Text

DS

The body or text is the message the writer wishes to convey to the reader of the report. The message begins with a short statement of what the report is about; that is, its purpose.

The body is usually divided into subsections preceded by headings that provide a road map that organizes the material and guides the reader through the message. Three levels of headings are often used.

DS

Main heading. The main heading of a report is the title which appears on the title page and reappears as the first line of the first page of the body of short reports. Because it is the most important heading, it is shown in ALL-CAP letters.

At least 1" or 6 lines

Page 1 of Unbound Report Manuscript

Page 2 of Unbound Report Manuscript

Report Documentation

Few people prepare reports "off the tops of their heads." Rather, they depend upon the writing of others for facts and ideas. When the work of others is used to add support and credibility to a paper, credit should be given to the sources used. This process of giving credit is called *documentation*. Three methods for documenting are widely used: footnotes/bibliography, endnotes, and textual citations/reference list.

In the past the footnotes/bibliography method was most widely used. This method requires the use of superior (raised) footnote reference figures at appropriate points within the text with matching-number footnotes at the foot of the page on which the reference figures appear. At the end of such a report, all references cited in the footnotes (plus relevant general references) are arranged alphabetically by author names on a separate page for easy reference. In this plan, estimating space to be left for footnotes is difficult; adding or deleting footnotes requires retyping the copy; and retyping footnotes in a different format to create the bibliography adds needless work.

A simpler system called endnote referencing was adopted by the Modern Language Association to eliminate the disadvantages of the footnoting system. In the endnote method, superior reference figures are used within the text (as for footnotes), but the number-matched notes are listed numerically at the end of the paper or report.

Increasing use of electronic word processing equipment, some of which cannot "raise" the superior reference figures, has led to increasing use of a documentation system called textual citations/reference list or within-text author/date citations. This system is described under the topic "Reference Citations" on page 6 and is illustrated in the model report on page 7. When within-text author/date citations are used, a reference list on a separate page at the end of the report provides in alphabetic order by author names the complete reference information.

New editions of reference guides and handbooks for writers are increasingly featuring and recommending the use of the textual citations/reference list method of documentation. For this reason and because this book is designed for use with computers, all reports will use this system of documentation.

Formatting the Reference List (Bibliography)

The reference list or bibliography page uses the same placement and spacing guides as those used for the first page of an unbound report: 1″ side margins; the heading REFERENCES on line 10 (pica or 10-pitch); or line 12 (elite or 12-pitch); bottom margin of *at least* 1 inch.

The first entry of the reference list or bibliography begins at the left margin a quadruple space (QS) or on the fourth line space below the heading. The lines of each entry are single-spaced; a double space is left between entries. The second line and subsequent lines of individual entries are indented 5 spaces from the left margin.

Entries are arranged alphabetically by author surnames. A reference that does not show an author name is listed alphabetically by the first important word in its title (articles are excluded). Proper sequence, capitalization, punctuation, and spacing of reference list entries are illustrated in the model on the facing page and below.

One-Author Book
Frosch, Alice. Report Style. Springfield, MA: Julius Publishing Co., 1985.

Two- or Three-Author Book
Richards, Paul A., Janet L. Miggs, and Jay W. Fritz. Modern Office Systems. 2d ed. Chicago: Bryson and Kline, Publishers, 1984.

Editor-as-"Author" Book
Tillotson, Margaret, ed. Computers as Word Processors: Pros and Cons. San Jose: InfoComp, Inc., 1983.

Magazine Article
Taylor, Orin. "Why Don't They Standardize Computer Keyboards?" Computer Periscope, October 1985, 34-36.

Newspaper Article
Lopez, Juanita. "Secretarily Speaking." The Cincinnati Globe, 22 March 1983, E12.

Formatting the Title Page

The content of the title or cover page consists of the report title; the name of the writer; the name of the school, business, or organization; and the month, day, and year the report was completed.

To reduce the number of uses of the RETURN required to space from part to part, set the machine for double-spacing mode. With a word processor, you can continue single spacing and use codes to insert blank lines.

The *title* of the report is centered in ALL-CAP letters on the 16th line (8 double spaces) from the top edge of the page. If the title requires more than one line, double-space the lines.

The *name of the writer* is centered in capital-and-lowercase letters on line 32 (the 16th line below the report title). The name of the school, department, business, or organization is centered in capital-and-lowercase letters a double space below the writer's name on line 34.

The *date* is centered on line 50 (the 16th line below the writer's school, department, business, or organization name).

> All reports in this book consist of a title page, two or three pages of text, and a reference list.

List of References for Unbound Report

1"

In single-space (SS) mode, enter heading on line 10.

Leave 3 blank line spaces.

REFERENCES

House, Clifford, and Kathie Sigler. Reference Manual for Office Personnel. 6th ed. Cincinnati: South-Western Publishing Co., 1981.

DS

Pasewark, William R., and Mary Ellen Oliverio. Procedures for the Modern Office. 7th ed. Cincinnati: South-Western Publishing Co., 1983.

Seybold, Catharine, and Bruce Young. The Chicago Manual of Style. 13th ed. Chicago: The University of Chicago Press, 1982.

Wolf, Morris, and Shirley Kuiper. Effective Communication in Business. 8th ed. Cincinnati: South-Western Publishing Co., 1984.

1"

Title Page of Unbound Report

Enter title on line 16.

THREE MAJOR PARTS OF SHORT REPORTS

Enter name on line 32 (leave 15 blank line spaces).

Marjorie Brooks   DS
Delta Business Academy

Enter date on line 50 (leave 15 blank line spaces).

October 12, 19--

PART 1
COMPUTER-FORMATTED UNBOUND REPORTS

On pages 16-21 are two unbound reports that you will key: Report 1 and Report 2. Each report is divided into two assignments:

Assignment A: The *body* of the report.
Assignment B: The *references* and *title page*.

For example, Report 1A refers to the body of the first report. Report 1B refers to the references and title page of the same report.

You will use Disk 1 to key these four computer-formatted exercises. As you key the exercises, you will be shown how the reports should be formatted. You will be prompted to key each part of the report, and the computer will format it automatically.

Screen Format

You will use the microcomputer in much the same way as a typewriter (not a word processor). However, the text you key will appear on the screen, not on paper, and you will print it at a later time.

When you begin a computer-formatted exercise, your microcomputer screen will look like the following display.

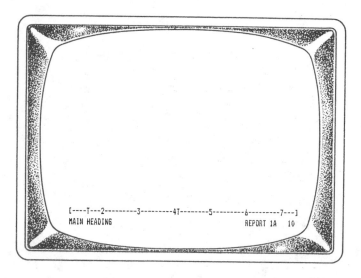

[----T---2---------3--------4T------5--------6---------7---]
MAIN HEADING   REPORT 1A   10

Format line. When you key a computer-formatted exercise, there will be a format line on the next to last line of the screen. This format line is similar to the line-of-writing scale on a typewriter. The square brackets at either end of the format line indicate the left and right margins that have been set for the exercise. In the screen above, the margins are set at 10 and 74.

Each digit in the format line represents ten spaces. For example, the "2" appears in Column 20 and the "3" appears in Column 30. A "T" in the format line indicates that a tab has been set at that position.

You can use this format line to determine your current position on a line. There is a solid white block, called a cursor, on the screen whenever you key text. This cursor indicates your current position on the screen. If, for instance, the cursor is directly above the "2," you are at position 20. This means that when you print the document, the character that you entered at that position will be in Column 20 on the paper.

Command line. The bottom line of the screen is called the command line. The command line consists of the following three parts:

(1) *Prompt.* At the left of the command line is the prompt that tells you what part of the report to key. In the preceding display, the prompt is "MAIN HEADING." This means that you should key the main heading of the report.

(2) *Exercise title.* The exercise title appears next in the command line. The title for the exercise shown is "REPORT 1A."

(3) *Line indicator.* The line indicator (10 in the screen shown) is at the right of the command line. This tells you your current line. For instance, if the line indicator reads "10," the text you key will be on line 10 of the printed report.

Scrolling. You begin keying text at the bottom of the screen above the format line. Each time you begin a new line of text, the entered text scrolls up one line for single spacing or two lines for double spacing, just as the paper scrolls up in a typewriter. Once the text reaches the top of the screen, the beginning lines of text scroll off the screen one at a time. Although you cannot see this text on the screen, it will appear when you print the assignment.

Using the Keyboard

Before keying the computer-formatted exercises, you need to learn how to use the keyboard. The keys on the keyboard of your computer are similar in position to the keys on a typewriter. However, there are a few differences.

Spacing. Spacing is achieved in the same way on the screen as it is on a typewriter. The *space bar, backspace key, carriage return key,* and *tab key* are used to position print on the paper. A *tone or end-of-line bar* is used to warn you that you are within five spaces of the right margin.

- *Space bar.* The space bar moves the cursor one space to the right until the end of the line is reached.
- *Backspace key.* The backspace key moves the cursor one space to the left until the beginning of the line is reached.
- *Carriage return.* The carriage return key (RETURN on the Apple computer, ENTER on the TRS-80 and IBM computers) is used to indicate that you have completed a line. This key moves the cursor down one line and back to the left margin of the screen.
- *Tab key.* The tab key (TAB on the Apple computer, → on the TRS-80, and the Tab key on the IBM) is used to move the cursor to the next tab stop on the line. The tab stops are indicated in the format line at the bottom of the screen.
- *End-of-line bar or tone.* When you reach the position five spaces before the right margin, a warning is issued to let you know that you are nearing the end of the line. On the TRS-80 computer, a solid bar appears in the remaining spaces of the line. These characters are replaced by the characters you type. When you strike the carriage return key, the remainder of the bar disappears. On the Apple and IBM computers, a tone sounds to warn you that five spaces remain on the line.

Commands. There are a few commands that use keys normally available on a typewriter. These special commands are used for the following operations: *caps lock, erase, overstriking, margin release,* and *underlining.* Some of these commands require holding down the Control key and striking a lowercase letter key. On the Apple, IBM, and TRS-80 Model 4 computers, the key labeled CTRL is the control key. On the TRS-80 Model III computer, the Shift key and down-arrow key, used together, are the Control key. A command using a Control key is represented by a letter in angle brackets. For instance, the symbol <R>, called Control-R, means "hold down the Control key and strike R."

- *Caps lock.* The caps lock command will allow you to key text in capital letters without having to hold down the Shift key. The way you turn on the caps lock depends on which computer you are using.

    Apple, IBM, and TRS-80 Model 4: depress the Caps Lock key.

    TRS-80 Model III: hold down the Shift key and strike 0 (zero).

    The procedure for turning off caps lock is the same as for turning it on.

    Whether the caps lock is on or off, you must always hold down the Shift key to type all non-

alphabetic keys for which the Shift key is normally used. For example, parentheses always require the Shift key.

- *Erase <E>.* Corrections may be made on the line on which you are working. Once you proceed to another line, you cannot make corrections in the previous line. To make a correction, use the backspace key or the space bar to position the cursor over the character you want to erase. Hold down the Control key and strike E (on the Apple and IBM computers you may simply strike the delete key). The character is erased and a blank space remains. You may now type over the blank space with a new character.
- *Overstriking.* By moving the cursor to any blank space on a line, you can replace the space with a character. Like erasing, overstriking can be used on the current line only. You are not allowed to overstrike one character with another. The character must be erased before a new character can be displayed.
- *Margin release <R>.* Control-R is used to release the right margin. You can use this command at any point in a line to type beyond the right margin of the current line. Although you can type beyond the right margin, you are always limited to 64 characters. Therefore, if the right margin minus the left margin equals 64, the margin release will not allow you to key any more characters on that line.
- *Underlining <L>.* The microcomputer cannot display underlined text on the screen. However, you can use a special command, Control-L, to signal the computer that you want that text to be underlined in the final copy.

    To underline text, use the following procedures:
    (1) Position the cursor in the *space before* the first word to be underlined.
    (2) Hold down the Control key and strike L. The backslash symbol (\ ) will appear in the space.
    (3) Key the text to be underlined.
    (4) Hold down the Control key and strike L. Another slash will appear in the *space after* the last word to be underlined.

The slashes should be entered in the spaces between words. When the document is printed, the text between the slashes will be underlined. The slashes will be removed, and spaces will appear instead.

Example:

Screen Text: \The Cat in the Hat\ was written by Dr. Seuss.

Printed Text: The Cat in the Hat was written by Dr. Seuss.

If underlined text continues from one line to another, you can enter the first slash on one line and the second slash on another, and all text in between will be underlined. (References are an exception; see page 13.)

There are a few cases in which there is no space before or after text to enter a slash:

(1) When the first word to be underlined is at the left margin.
(2) When the first word to be underlined is preceded by a parenthesis.
(3) When the last word to be underlined is followed by punctuation or a parenthesis.

In these cases you should still enter the slashes before and after the appropriate text. The slashes and the extra spaces will be removed automatically during printing.

Example:

Screen Text: "A/R" is the correct abbreviation for "account receivable" (\American Heritage Dictionary\, 1980).

Printed Text: "A/R" is the correct abbreviation for "account receivable" (American Heritage Dictionary, 1980).

Remember that in order for underlining to work correctly, the printer must be able to backspace. If your printer does not backspace, it is recommended that you omit the underlines. Book titles should be keyed in all-caps if you cannot underline them.

Special commands. There are three special commands that do not exist on a typewriter: an *execute* command, a *help* command, and an *escape* command.

- *Execute <X>.* You are prompted to enter each part of a report in the computer-formatted exercises. After you finish keying each part of the report, you must strike Control-X. This signals the computer to issue the next prompt and to move the cursor to the next position.

- *Help <Z>.* At any time while you are keying a computer-formatted exercise, you may strike Control-Z, and the bottom two lines of the screen will be replaced with a summary of the commands you may use. When you have finished looking at the command summary, strike RETURN/ENTER, and the previous two lines will reappear.

- *Escape.* If you wish to exit without completing an exercise, you may strike ESC (Apple or IBM) or CLEAR (TRS-80). You will be given the opportunity to confirm or cancel the escape command. The exercise cannot be saved if you use the escape command.

Completing a Computer-Formatted Exercise

Selecting the assignment. Each time you begin a computer-formatted exercise, follow these procedures:

(1) Sign on to the computer using Disk 1 for Module A (see page 3).
(2) At the Main Menu, key the number 1 and strike RETURN/ENTER for the computer-formatted exercises.
(3) At the next menu, titled "Computer-Formatted Exercises," key the number 1 and strike RETURN/ENTER to enter a document.
(4) At the Module Menu, key the appropriate number and strike RETURN/ENTER for the appropriate exercise.

Keying the assignment. The computer prompts you for each part of the report. For instance, for Report 1A, the body of the report, you are given the following prompts:

Main heading
Introductory paragraph
First side heading
Side heading paragraph
Second side heading
Side heading paragraph
First paragraph heading and paragraph
Page number (for second page of report)
Second paragraph heading and paragraph
Third paragraph heading and paragraph
Third side heading
Side heading paragraph

For Report 1B, the following prompts are given for the references:

Reference title
First source
Second source
Third source
Fourth source

These are followed by prompts for the title page:

Title
Name of writer
School
Date

The cursor is positioned at the appropriate line and column automatically. You need only key the text and the report will be formatted for you. The line indicator and format line show you the correct position for each part of the report.

NOTE: Some assignments require you to enter your own name and school and the current date. Because these entries will vary with each student, the computer positions the cursor at the center point. You must backspace one space for every two characters to center each entry.

Key the report, part by part, using the commands described previously. Enter the copy line for line and page for page as shown in the assignment. Strike Control-X when you finish each part of the report. Remember that you can see on the screen a summary of the available commands by striking Control-Z.

- *Notes concerning underlining.* The slashes on either side of underlined text should be entered in the spaces between words. When a prompt for a paragraph heading is given, the cursor will be indented automatically five positions from the left margin. Backspace one position to enter the slash, then key the text.

  A similar situation occurs with the references of a report. The first line of each source is keyed at the left margin, and each line following the first is indented five spaces. In this situation, if underlined text continues from one line to the next, you should end the underlining on the first line (by striking Control-L to enter a slash) and begin it again on the second line. The cursor will be automatically indented five spaces for the second line. You should backspace once to enter the slash in the preceding space.

  Example:

  Burtness, Paul S. \Effective English\
  \for Colleges\. 6th ed.   Cincinnati:
  South-Western Publishing Co., 1981.

- *Note concerning indenting.* If a prompt requires you to enter more than one paragraph, the cursor will be automatically indented for the first paragraph only. To indent the following paragraphs, you will need to strike the tab key (preset to indent five spaces).

Using the Functions Menu. When you strike Control-X after keying the last part of the assignment, the Computer-Formatted Functions Menu will appear on the screen.

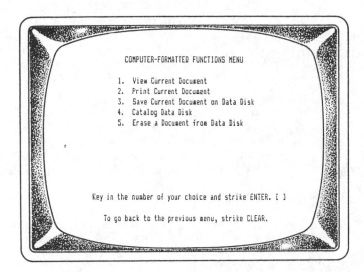

At this point you should use the following procedures:

(1) *Save the document.* If you are using a data disk, you should save the document. If you are not using a data disk, go to Step 2. To save the document, follow these procedures:

(a) Key the number 3 and strike RETURN/ENTER. You will be prompted to insert the data disk. If you have two disk drives, insert the data disk in the second drive. If you have one disk drive, remove the Report Formatting disk and insert the data disk.

(b) You will receive a screen instructing you to enter a document name. Key a document name and strike RETURN/ENTER. Recommended names are given in the directions for each document. You are allowed eight characters with no spaces for a document name. For example, for the first exercise, you should key the name REP1A.

(c) You will receive a message telling you that the document is being saved.

(2) *View the document.* Key the number 1 and strike RETURN/ENTER. Hold down the ↓ key to scroll down to line 10 to display the beginning of the document you keyed. Continue to use the ↓ key to view the remainder of the document, or use the ↑ key if you wish to scroll back to look again at an earlier part. If your document is more than one page, continue to press the ↓ key to the bottom of each page. The page will be ejected automatically after line 66 to display the next page. Continue pressing the ↓ key to view the text on that page. When you have finished viewing the document, strike Control-Q to return to the Computer-Formatted Functions Menu. (After you have completed a few computer-formatted exercises,

you may choose to omit the step of viewing the document.)

(3) *Print the document.* If you have a printer attached to your microcomputer, follow these steps:

(a) Make sure the printer is properly prepared.
(b) Key the number 2 and strike RETURN/ENTER. The document will begin printing. A separate document identification page with your name, the date, and the name of the document will be printed after the document.

If you do not have a printer attached to your microcomputer, follow the steps below. Remember, you must have saved your document on a data disk in order to print it using another microcomputer.

(a) Strike ESC/CLEAR to go back to the previous menu.
(b) You will receive the message "If you go back to the previous menu, the current document will be cleared." Strike RETURN/ENTER. (The document will be cleared from the computer's memory, but it will still be saved on the data disk.)
(c) If you are using one disk drive, follow the directions to remove the data disk and insert the Report Formatting disk (the program disk). If you are using two disk drives, go to Step d.
(d) Continue striking ESC/CLEAR at each screen to move to the title screen.
(e) Remove the disks from the disk drives.
(f) Take the disks to a computer with a printer attached and insert the Report Formatting disk.
(g) Proceed to the Main Menu; select option 1 for Computer-Formatted Exercises.
(h) At the Computer-Formatted Exercises Menu, select item 2, Retrieve Document from Data Disk.
(i) Follow the instructions to insert the data disk.
(j) Follow the instructions to key the document name. Key the name exactly as you did when you saved the document. You will not see the document but a message will tell you that the document is being retrieved. The Computer-Formatted Functions Menu will appear.
(k) Make sure the printer is properly prepared.
(l) Key the number 2 and strike RETURN/ENTER to print the document. A separate document identification page with your name, the date, and the title of the document will be printed after the document.

Other functions. There are two functions listed on the Computer-Formatted Functions Menu that you may need to use occasionally: (1) Catalog Data Disk, and (2) Erase a Document from Data Disk.

• *Catalog Data Disk.* This function enables you to see the names of all documents saved on the data disk. You can use this function if you need to check what documents you saved or what names you used. To catalog the data disk, select function 4 and strike RETURN/ENTER. You will receive a screen like the following. (The format will vary slightly with different computers.)

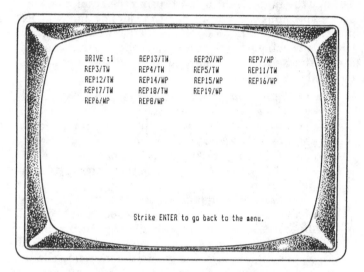

This catalog lists the name of every document saved in computer-formatted exercises, typewriter simulation, and word processor simulation. (On the TRS-80 version, there may also be additional files that were copied in the process of creating your data disk. Such files will not affect your work and may be ignored.) Each document is listed in the catalog with the document name and the type of simulation, separated by a period or a slash. The following two-letter codes are used to indicate the type of simulation:

CF   computer-formatted exercises
TW   typewriter simulation
WP   word processor simulation

After you have finished viewing the catalog, strike RETURN/ENTER to go back to the Computer-Formatted Functions Menu.

• *Erase a Document from Data Disk.* To erase a document from the data disk, select function 5 and strike RETURN/ENTER. You will be prompted to key the name of the document you want to erase. In case you have made a mistake, you will be prompted to confirm your request to erase the document by striking Y for yes or N for no, and striking RETURN/ ENTER. You will receive a message that the document is being erased.

Beginning Another Assignment

You may have time to complete more than one assignment in a session. You should not begin another exercise unless you can finish keying all of it, because you cannot begin a computer-formatted exercise in one session and finish it in another. If you wish to key another assignment, follow these procedures:

(1) At the Computer-Formatted Functions Menu, strike ESC/CLEAR to go back to the previous menu.

(2) You will receive the message "If you go back to the previous menu, the current document will be cleared." This is a reminder to you that unless you have saved the current document it will be lost. If you have not saved the document and wish to do so, strike ESC/CLEAR to cancel the request to go back to the previous menu. Otherwise, strike RETURN/ENTER.

(3) If you are using one disk drive, follow the instruction to switch disks. If you are using two disk drives, go on to step 4.

(4) You should be at the Computer-Formatted Exercises Menu. Follow the same procedures as before to select an exercise.

Repeating an Assignment

It is possible to repeat a computer-formatted exercise by following the same procedures as for the first time. If you wish to save the document, use the same name as for the first version, and the document will replace the first version on the data disk.

Exiting

To finish your session, follow these procedures:

(1) Follow the procedures described in the section "Beginning Another Assignment" to return to the Computer-Formatted Exercises Menu from the Computer-Formatted Functions Menu.

(2) Continue striking ESC/CLEAR to go back to the title screen.

(3) At the title screen, follow the procedures for "powering down" the computer.

Before beginning the report formatting assignments, be sure you have read the Introduction on pages 1-4, studied the formatting guides and model report on pages 6-9, and read the procedures on pages 10-15.

Report 1A

Key in the report shown at the right and on page 17. Wait for each prompt to appear on the display screen telling you what you are to do next. Enter the copy line for line and page for page as shown. Strike RETURN (ENTER) at the end of each line.

When you have finished, store the report on your data disk (if you are using one) under the name REP1A.

Print out a copy of your work.

You will prepare a reference page and a title page to complete the report.

THREE MAJOR PARTS OF SHORT REPORTS

Short reports consist of three major parts: a title page, the body or text, and a reference list or bibliography. Each of these parts is briefly described here in order of occurrence in a report.

Title Page

The title page or cover page gives the title of the report; the name of the writer; the name of the school, business, or organization for which the report was prepared; and the date on which the report was completed (House and Sigler, 1981, 181). The title page answers the important questions what, who, where, and when.

Body or Text

The body or text is the message the writer wishes to convey to the reader of the report. The message begins with a short statement of what the report is about; that is, its purpose. The body is usually divided into subsections preceded by headings that provide a road map that organizes the material and guides the reader through the message. Three levels of headings are often used.

Main heading. The main heading of a report is the title which appears on the title page and reappears as the first line of the first page of the body of short reports. Because it is the most important heading, it is shown in ALL-CAP letters.

Report 1A continues on page 17.

2

   Side headings. Side headings show the major subdivisions
of the main heading or topic. They announce the main ideas of
the report message. They appear in capital-and-lowercase letters at the left margin with a blank line space left above and
below them. Because of their importance, they are underlined.
Placing them on separate lines and underlining them give them
emphasis.

   Paragraph headings. Paragraph headings indicate further
subdivisions of the main ideas represented by the side headings. They are indented as part of the first line of the para
graph, are underlined, and end with a period. Only the first
word and proper names are capitalized in paragraph headings.

Reference List

   The list of references used in compiling the report is the
last page of most reports, except for long reports that have appendices or an index. The reference list, sometimes called a
bibliography, together with author/date/page citations within
the body of the report are called the report's documentation.
All references cited within the report must appear in the reference list (Seybold and Young, 1982, 420). Other references used
for verifying information may also be included. The reference
list should not be "padded." On the other hand, it should be
sufficient to lend credibility to the content of the report.

References and Title Page appear on page 18.

Report 1B

Reference List

Enter the list of references line for line as shown at the right. The reference list will be a separate page at the end of the report.

Next, enter the title page as directed below.

REFERENCES

House, Clifford, and Kathie Sigler. Reference Manual for Office Personnel. 6th ed. Cincinnati: South-Western Publishing Co., 1981.

Pasewark, William R., and Mary Ellen Oliverio. Procedures for the Modern Office. 7th ed. Cincinnati: South-Western Publishing Co., 1983.

Seybold, Catharine, and Bruce Young. The Chicago Manual of Style. 13th ed. Chicago: The University of Chicago Press, 1982.

Wolf, Morris, and Shirley Kuiper. Effective Communication in Business. 8th ed. Cincinnati: South-Western Publishing Co., 1984.

Title Page

Enter the information for a title page as the computer prompts you, part by part.

When you are finished, store the reference list and title page on your data disk (if you are using one) under the name REP1B.

Print out a copy of your work.

Finally, assemble the four pages: title page, two pages of text, and reference list. Staple them across the upper lefthand corner. Your report will then be ready to present to your instructor.

Information for the title page

TITLE: THREE MAJOR PARTS OF SHORT REPORTS

NAME: Marjorie Brooks

SCHOOL: Delta Business Academy

DATE: October 12, 19--

Enter the copy shown at the right and on page 20 as two pages of an unbound report. Wait for each prompt to appear on the display screen telling you what you are to do next. Enter the copy line for line and page for page as shown.

When you have finished, store the report on your data disk (if you are using one) under the name REP2A.

Print out a copy of your work.

You will prepare a reference page and a title page to complete the report.

DOCUMENTING MANUSCRIPTS AND REPORTS

Many of the papers and reports prepared by students, business workers, and professional people depend upon the writing of others for facts and ideas. When the work of others is used to add support and credibility to a paper, credit should be given to the sources used. The process by which this is accomplished is called documentation. Three methods of documenting are used widely: footnote/bibliography, endnotes, and textual citations/ reference list.

Footnotes/Bibliography

The footnotes/bibliography method used to be the standard method for documenting a paper or report. It requires the use of superior (raised) footnote reference figures at appropriate points within the text with matching-number footnotes at the foot of the page on which the reference figures appear. At the end of such a report, all references cited in the footnotes (plus relevant general references) are arranged alphabetically on a separate page for easy reference. Turabian (1973, 132-143) uses this method.

In this plan, estimating space to be left for footnotes is difficult; adding or deleting footnotes requires retyping the copy; and rekeying footnotes in a different format to create the bibliography adds needless work. As a result, endnotes came into use.

Report 2A continues on page 20.

2

<u>Endnotes</u>

In the endnotes method, superior reference figures are used within the text (as for footnotes), but the number-matched notes are listed numerically at the end of the paper or report.

The endnote method, once recommended by the Modern Language Association (1977, 28-31), is simpler and less work than the footnote method. The inability of some modern electronic printers, used with computers, to "raise" the superior figures, however, has led to increased use of author-date citations within the text. The author-date method is used in this report.

<u>Textual Citations/Reference List</u>

The textual citation method of referencing is strongly recommended by Seybold and Young in <u>The Chicago Manual</u> (1982, 400). They consider it the most economical method "in space, in time, and in cost." In this method, the surname of each author, the date of publication, and page numbers of the material cited are given in the text. A list of references arranged alphabetically by author surnames appears at the end of the paper.

The author-date method of documentation is widely used in professional journals and textbooks, many of which are "typeset" by computer. Although older style manuals, such as Turabian's <u>A Manual for Writers</u>, 4th Edition, and the <u>MLA Handbook</u>, 1977 Edition, emphasize footnote/bibliography and endnote methods, both recognize the author-date method as an acceptable way to document papers and reports. The <u>APA Publication Manual</u> (1974, 58-59) recommends the author-date style, as does the new <u>MLA Handbook</u> (1984, 161-163).

References and Title Page appear on page 21.

Report 2B

Reference List

Enter the list of references line for line as shown at the right. The reference list will be a separate page at the end of the report.

Next, enter the title page as directed below.

NOTE: An underline at the beginning of a reference citation indicates that the author is the same as in the preceding entry. Type the underline the length of the author's last name (in this listing, 7 spaces) and follow it with a period. If your computer printer cannot print underlines, use hyphens in place of the underline.

REFERENCES

APA Publication Manual. 2d ed. Washington, DC: American
     Psychological Association, 1974.

Gibaldi, Joseph, and Walter S. Achtert. MLA Handbook for Writ-
     ers of Research Papers, Theses, and Dissertations. New
     York: Modern Language Association, 1977.

_____. MLA Handbook for Writers of Research Papers. 2d
     ed. New York: Modern Language Association, 1984.

Seybold, Catharine, and Bruce Young. The Chicago Manual of
     Style. 13th ed. Chicago: The University of Chicago
     Press, 1982.

Turabian, Kate L. A Manual for Writers of Term Papers, Theses,
     and Dissertations. 4th ed. Chicago: The University of
     Chicago Press, 1973.

Title Page

Enter the information for a title page as the computer prompts you, part by part.

When you are finished, store the reference list and title page on your data disk (if you are using one) under the name REP2B.

Print out a copy of your work.

Finally, assemble the four pages: title page, two pages of text, and reference list. Staple them across the upper lefthand corner. Your report will then be ready to present to your instructor.

Information for the title page

TITLE: DOCUMENTING MANUSCRIPTS AND REPORTS

NAME: Francisco Duarte

SCHOOL: Midwest Institute of Journalism

DATE: May 14, 19--

PART 2
TYPEWRITER SIMULATION: UNBOUND REPORTS

On pages 27-35 are three unbound reports for you to key using the typewriter simulation: Report 3, Report 4, and Report 5. For each report, you will key the body, the references, then the title page.

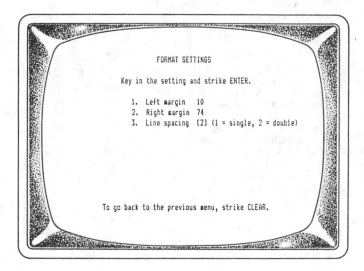

Formatting with the Typewriter Simulation

You will make your own formatting decisions as you key reports with the typewriter simulation. You will set margins and tabs, and determine the placement of all parts of a report. Format the reports according to the same guidelines you learned for computer-formatted exercises. If you have any questions concerning formatting rules, refer back to the Formatting Guides on pages 6-9.

In this simulation, as with a typewriter, you will use a manual procedure for centering headings.

(1) Tabulate to center of paper.
(2) From center, backspace once for each 2 characters (letter, space, figure, symbol, or punctuation mark) in the line to be centered. To do this: Say the characters in pairs, as CE NT ER; backspace once for each pair. If an odd or leftover stroke is left at the end of a line, do not backspace for it.

(3) Begin the heading where the backspacing ends.

Using the Microcomputer as a Typewriter

Format settings. When you create a document using the typewriter simulation, you begin by determining the format settings for the document. As with a typewriter, you set the left margin, right margin, and line spacing before beginning the document. However, rather than setting the margins and line spacing mechanically, as on a typewriter, you key the settings at the screen titled "Format Settings."

You should follow these procedures at the Format Setting screen:

(1) Key the left margin and strike RETURN/ENTER. For unbound reports, you should have a left margin of one inch or 10 pica spaces. Therefore, key 10 for this setting. (There is a minimum left margin setting of 3 in this typewriter simulation.)

(2) Key the right margin and strike RETURN/ENTER. Unbound reports would ordinarily have a right margin of one inch or 10 pica spaces. However, because some microcomputer screens are limited to 64-character lines, the right margin setting minus the left margin setting cannot be greater than 64. Therefore, you should set the right margin at 74. This will give you a right margin of just over one inch. (There is a maximum right margin setting of 82; also, the right margin minus the left margin must be at least 20.)

(3) Key the setting for line spacing and strike RETURN/ENTER. The setting for single spacing is "1"; for double spacing the setting is "2." The body of an unbound report should be double spaced. For references and the title page, you will change the line spacing to "1." After keying all the format settings, you will be prompted to accept or change the settings.

"**Rolling in the paper.**" After you determine the format settings, you will receive a screen, like the following one, with a format line, a line indicator, and the message "Strike RETURN" or "Strike ENTER."

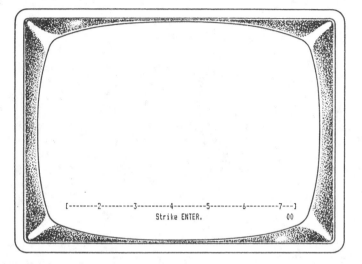

The format line for the typewriter simulation is the same as for computer-formatted exercises, beginning at the left margin (see explanation on page 10). Notice in the screen above that the margins are set at 10 and 74. Notice also that the line indicator reads "00." This indicates that "the paper" has not yet been "rolled into the typewriter." Use the following procedures to roll in the paper.

(1) Strike RETURN/ENTER. Notice that the line indicator now reads "02." This means that you are on the second line of the "paper." (If you were in single-space mode, the line indicator would read "01.")

(2) Continue striking RETURN/ENTER until you are at the appropriate line to begin typing. For unbound reports the title or main heading on the first page appears on line 10. Therefore, you should strike RETURN/ENTER until the line indicator reads "10." Check the Formatting Guides on pages 6 and 8 to determine where to begin typing on other pages of an unbound report.

Setting/clearing/purging tabs. You should set tabs before you begin typing the document. For an unbound report, you should set tabs at 16 (for indenting paragraphs), and 42 (for tabbing to the center). You will also tab to position 74, the right margin, to key page numbers, but you do not need to set a tab there (the right margin operates as a tab stop). To set a tab, strike the space bar until the cursor is above the appropriate position in the format line and strike Control-S.

You can set additional tabs or revise tabs at any time while keying a document. To clear a tab, space to the position of the tab you want to clear, and strike Control-C. To clear all tabs at once (purge), strike Control-P with the cursor at any point.

Using the Keyboard

In the typewriter simulation, you can use most of the same commands that you used to key the computer-formatted exercises. You already have been introduced to the following commands:

- space bar
- backspace
- carriage return
- tab key
- caps lock
- margin release
- underlining

Refer to pages 11-12 if you want to review these commands.

Because you will be doing your own formatting in the typewriter simulation, there are commands in addition to those listed above that you will use.

Scrolling. You can scroll up or down on a "page" while using the typewriter simulation. To scroll down line by line, press the carriage return key as you would on a typewriter. To scroll up, strike the ↑ key.

Erase <E>. To erase a character, position the cursor using the space bar or the ←key, and strike Control-E (or the Delete key on the Apple and IBM computers), as you learned for computer-formatted exercises. In the typewriter simulation, you may erase an error on any line by scrolling to the appropriate line, positioning the cursor, and using the erase command.

New page <N>. If the document you are typing is more than one page long, you will need to "eject" each "page" before going on to the next. The recommended bottom margin for unbound reports is one inch. Therefore, line 60 should be the last line on which you type text. When you reach line 60, a tone will sound on the Apple and IBM microcomputers, and the line indicator will flash on the TRS-80 microcomputer. This is to remind you to eject the page. After you key the text on line 60, eject the page by striking Control-N. The page of text will scroll off the screen automatically, and you will be ready to start a new page. Remember to strike RETURN/ENTER the appropriate number of times for a top margin for the next page.

There are a total of 66 lines on a page. Therefore, you will not be allowed to type beyond line 66 without ejecting the page. If you forget to eject a page, you will receive a reminder message at the end of line 66.

You may retrieve a page after you eject it by using the upward scroll key (↑). After you have scrolled to the top of a page, you can continue scrolling to the bottom of the previous page by using the ↑ key.

Change format settings <F>. If you need to indent a passage or make another type of formatting change, you can change the margin settings or line spacing. For instance, if your report includes a lengthy quotation, you would want to indent and single-space the quotation. To change a format setting, strike Control-F when you reach the point in your document where the format changes. You will receive the Format Setting screen with your original settings filled in. Follow the instructions on the screen to change the settings and to return to the document.

Because of limitations of the computer screen, you may indent margins but not outdent them from their *original* settings. For instance, if your original margins are 10 and 74, you can indent them to 15 and 69, then outdent them again to 10 and 74. However, you cannot outdent the left margin to less than 10 or the right margin to more than 74.

Help <Z>. At any time while keying text, you may strike Control-Z to receive a summary of the commands available in the typewriter simulation. The command summary replaces the bottom two lines of your screen. When you have finished reviewing the commands, strike RETURN/ENTER and the previous two lines will reappear.

Quit <Q>. When you have finished keying your document, strike Control-Q. This accesses the Typewriter Functions Menu which enables you to save and/or print the document. You need not complete a document in one session with the typewriter simulation. Even if you have not completed a document, you can strike Control-Q and then save onto your data disk the part of the report that you have keyed. You will be able to finish your report in a later session.

Completing a Typewriter Assignment

Selecting the assignment. Each time you begin an assignment with the typewriter simulation, follow these procedures:

(1) Sign on to the computer using Disk 1 for Module A (see page 3).
(2) At the Main Menu, key the number 2 and strike RETURN/ENTER for the typewriter simulation.
(3) At the Typewriter Functions Menu, key 1 and strike RETURN/ENTER for the function Create or Edit Document.

Keying the assignment. Use the following procedures to key the assignment, entering copy line for line and page for page as shown in the assignment.

(1) Select format settings for your document (see page 22). For unbound reports use the following settings:
    Left margin: 10
    Right margin: 74
    Line spacing: 2
(2) Using the procedures for the typewriter simulation, roll the paper in (page 23).
(3) Set tabs (page 23). For unbound reports, set tabs at 16 and 42.
(4) Key the first page of the report and eject the page.
(5) Key the second page of the report and eject the page.
(6) Access the format screen by striking Control-F and change the line spacing to "1" for single spacing the references.
(7) Key the references and eject the page.
(8) Key the title page.
(9) Strike Control-Q when finished. You will return to the Typewriter Functions Menu.

Using the document management functions. After you finish keying a document and return to the Typewriter Functions Menu, follow these procedures:

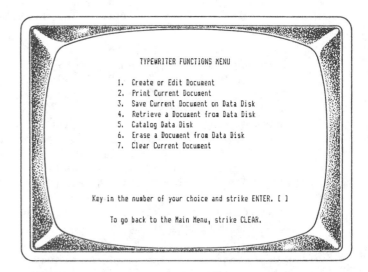

```
          TYPEWRITER FUNCTIONS MENU

    1.  Create or Edit Document
    2.  Print Current Document
    3.  Save Current Document on Data Disk
    4.  Retrieve a Document from Data Disk
    5.  Catalog Data Disk
    6.  Erase a Document from Data Disk
    7.  Clear Current Document



 Key in the number of your choice and strike ENTER. [ ]

 To go back to the Main Menu, strike CLEAR.
```

(1) *Save the document.* If you are using a data disk, save the document. If you are not using a data disk, go on to Step 2. To save the document, select function 3 and follow the directions on the screen. The Typewriter Functions Menu will remain on the screen as the document is saved.

(2) *Print the document.* If you have a printer attached to your microcomputer, follow these steps:
(a) Make sure the printer is properly prepared.
(b) Select function 2, Print Current Document. Your document will print, along with a separate document identification page with your name, the date, and the name of your document (if you saved it). After the document prints, you will still be at the Typewriter Functions Menu.

If you do not have a printer attached to your microcomputer, follow the steps below. Remember you must save the document before printing it on another microcomputer.
(a) Exit to the title screen and remove the disks.
(b) Take the disks to a computer with a printer attached and insert the Report Formatting disk.
(c) Proceed to the Typewriter Functions Menu.
(d) Retrieve the document by selecting function 4 and following the directions on the screen. You will not see the document but you will receive a message telling you that the document is being retrieved.
(e) Make sure the printer is properly prepared.
(f) Select function 2 to print the document.

Other functions. There are four functions on the Typewriter Functions Menu that you may use occasionally: Retrieve a Document from Data Disk, Catalog Data Disk, Erase a Document from Data Disk, and Clear Current Document.

• *Retrieve Document from Data Disk.* You can retrieve a document that you have saved on your data disk by selecting function 4 from the Typewriter Functions Menu. Once you have cleared a document from the computer's memory, you must retrieve it from your data disk in order to work with it again. Then you may view it, edit it, or print it.

• *Catalog Data Disk.* You can catalog the data disk by selecting function 5 from the Typewriter Functions Menu. Just as in the computer-formatted exercises, this function will provide you with a list of the names of all documents stored on the data disk.

• *Erase a Document from Data Disk.* You can erase a document that you created previously in any of the simulations by selecting function 6 and following the directions on the screen. Use this function if your data disk becomes full or if you want to remove documents that you no longer want on the data disk.

• *Clear Current Document.* If you have created or retrieved a document, you must clear the document from the computer's memory before you can create or retrieve another document. For instance, if you create, save, and print a document, you must clear the document from the computer's memory before you can create another. If you retrieve, edit, and save a document, you also must clear that document before retrieving or creating another. To clear a document, select function 7 and follow the directions on the screen. In order to protect the document in case you selected function 7 accidentally, you will be prompted to confirm this selection.

Finishing an Assignment in Another Session

You can start an assignment in one session and finish it in another with the typewriter simulation. If you have a data disk and want to do so, follow these procedures:

(1) When you want to stop keying the document, strike Control-Q to return to the Typewriter Functions Menu.
(2) Save the document on the data disk.
(3) Exit to the title screen and power down the computer.
(4) At the next session, proceed to the Typewriter Functions Menu.
(5) Retrieve the document from the data disk.
(6) Select function 1 to continue the document.
(7) Strike Control-N to move through any pages that you have already keyed.
(8) Strike RETURN/ENTER to move to the appropriate line for keying text.

If you would like to finish an exercise in another session but do not have a data disk on which to store your document, follow these procedures:

(1) When you want to stop keying the document, strike Control-Q to return to the Typewriter Functions Menu. Key to the end of a page before you end the session.
(2) Print the document.
(3) Exit to the title screen and power down the computer.
(4) At the next session, proceed to the Typewriter Functions Menu.
(5) Select Function 1 to create a document.
(6) Begin keying at the point where you left off, preferably at the beginning of a page.

Beginning Another Assignment

After you complete an assignment, you may want to start another. If so, follow these procedures:

(1) At the Typewriter Functions Menu, select function 7 to clear the current document, then follow the directions on the screen.
(2) After the document has been cleared, select function 1 Create or Edit Document.
(3) Follow the same procedures as before to create the new document.

Editing a Document

You may edit any typewriter simulation document that you have saved on the data disk by following these procedures:

(1) Retrieve the document from the data disk.
(2) Select function 1 to edit the document. You will bypass the Format Setting screen and go directly to the document.
(3) Edit the document using the commands available in the typewriter simulation.
(4) Strike Control-Q to return to the Typewriter Functions Menu.
(5) Save the revised document. Use the same name as you did for the first version, and the revised document will replace the earlier version on the data disk.
(6) Print the revised document, if desired.

Proofreader's Marks

Some of the reports are presented to you in script and typewritten rough-draft form as they would come to you in an office. Refer, when necessary, to the list of proofreader's marks below.

Mark	Meaning
Cap or ≡	Capitalize
⌒	Close up
ℓ	Delete
∧	Insert
⋏	Insert comma
# or /#	Insert space
∨	Insert apostrophe
⋎⋎ ⋎⋎	Insert quotation marks
⊐	Move right
⊏	Move left
⊔	Move down; lower
⊓	Move up; raise
lc or /	Set in lowercase
¶	Paragraph
no new ¶	No new paragraph
‖	Set flush; align type
sp	Spell out
stet	Let it stand; ignore correction
∿ or tr	Transpose
———	Underline or Italics

Before beginning the following
report formatting assignments,
be sure you have read the formatting guides on pages 6-9. Be
sure, also, that you have studied
the material on pages 22-26
which explains how to use the
typewriter simulation.

Report 3

Key in the report line for line and
page for page as shown at the
right and on page 28. You, not
the computer, are responsible
for centering headings and for
spacing properly between report
parts.

When you have finished the
two pages, make any necessary
corrections. Then proceed to
page 29 and key in the reference
page and the title page.

THE OFFICE TELEPHONE

The use of the telephone in the office is so routine today
that it is hard to believe that the first telephone exchange was
opened just over a hundred years ago. At the turn of the century, the letter was the primary means of office communication
even though the telegraph was used for quick contact over long
distances. Before long, though, business firms began to recognize the merits of a network of telephones.

Initially, the telephone system was a private rather than a
public one. Companies set up direct lines between their offices
and major clients and with sources of data, such as a stock mar-
ket. As the use of the telephone grew, however, the telephones
within many cities were connected by a central exchange attended
by operators. The network grew as increasing numbers of cities
were linked together by cable, but it was not until just before
World War I that the first coast-to-coast call was made (Encyclopedia Americana, 1979, 399).

Great progress in technology was needed to supply the growing demand for telephone service. The dial phone eliminated the
need for an operator on many calls. The coaxial cable, which
can carry a large number of circuits, took the place of individual lines. To meet a demand for even more service, a series
of radio relays was used for calls. By mating radio waves with
earth satellites, an intricate global telephone network was set

up (Popham et al., 1983, 311). We can now talk with others all over the world by merely pushing buttons.

A telephone system provides us with a great deal more than verbal contact between two points. Both our radio and our television networks rely heavily on telephone service. By the use of telephone wires, it is possible to send radio and television shows from the point of origin to distant and isolated places. If we did not have this service, many of us would not be able to enjoy national sports contests such as the Super Bowl or major events such as a special address by the President.

A special portable telephone which is known as a data phone serves many useful purposes. The phone can be used by a doctor to send data from the bedside of a patient to laboratories or specialists for immediate analysis. This service saves not only time but lives as well. The data phone can also be used to send or obtain data from centralized data banks of all kinds. When tied in with a computer, it can be used to process data and to solve many complex problems.

Business offices often have a variety of telephone devices. Data, reports, and documents of all kinds can be sent from place to place by the use of a picture phone. Telephone answering sets, which record messages on tape, can be used to answer the phone when no one is present (Pasewark and Oliverio, 1983, 213). Equipment of this type can also be used by out-of-town personnel to report and record sales. Similar devices are used by executives to dictate correspondence directly to a central word processing center.

Report 3, continued

Reference List

Enter the list of references line for line as shown at the right. Use single-space mode. DS between the entries.

    Make any necessary corrections, then key in the title page as directed below.

REFERENCES

Pasewark, William, and Mary Ellen Oliverio. <u>Procedures for the Modern Office</u>. 7th ed. Cincinnati: South-Western Publishing Co., 1983.

Popham, Estelle, Rita Tilton, Howard Jackson, and Marshall Hanna. <u>Secretarial Procedures and Administration</u>. 8th ed. Cincinnati: South-Western Publishing Co., 1983.

"Telephone." <u>Encyclopedia Americana</u>. Vol. 26. Danberry, CT: Encyclopedia Americana Corp., 1979.

Title Page

Enter the information for a title page. Be sure to center your name, the school name, and the date.

    Make any necessary corrections, then store the report on your data disk (if you are using one) as REP3. Print out a copy of the entire report.

    Finally, assemble the four pages: title page, two pages of text, and reference list. Staple them across the upper lefthand corner. Your report will then be ready to present to your instructor.

Information for the title page

TITLE: THE OFFICE TELEPHONE

NAME: Your own

SCHOOL: Your own

DATE: Current

WORK EVALUATION

To evaluate your work, answer the questions listed at the right. If your work does not meet acceptable standards, check with your instructor to see if you should revise the report and print out a new copy.

Self-Check Questions

                                                           Yes No   Yes No

1. Did you place the report title on line 10 from top of page? — —
2. Did you leave 3 blank line spaces between the title and the first line of the body? — —
3. Did you use DS mode for the body of the report? — —
4. Did you leave a bottom margin of at least 1 inch on each page? — —
5. Did you number page 2 at the right margin on line 6? — —
6. Did you begin the body of page 2 on line 8? — —
7. Are left and right margins approximately equal in width? — —
8. Did you enter the heading of the reference list on line 10? — —

9. Did you SS the items of the reference list? — —
10. Did you DS between the entries of the reference list? — —
11. Did you begin each reference list entry at the left margin and indent the other lines 5 spaces? — —
12. Are all book titles in the reference list underlined? — —
13. On the title page, did you enter the title on line 16? — —
14. Did you enter your name on line 32? — —
15. Did you DS between your name and the name of your school? — —
16. Did you enter the current date on line 50? — —

HEALTH INSURANCE

Report 4

Key in the report line for line and page for page as shown at the right and on page 31. You, not the computer, are responsible for placing and spacing the headings properly.

When you have finished the two pages and made any necessary corrections, proceed to page 32 and key in the reference page and the title page.

One of the fastest rising costs in the typical family's budget is the cost of health care. Between 1967 and 1979 health care costs rose almost 140% (Hodgetts, 1983, 378). Health care involves big money. "About $335 billion was spent in the U.S. in 1982 on health related expenditures" (Mathur, 1984, 374).

Since a major illness or injury could be financially devastating, it is imperative that each individual investigate the various health insurance plans that are available. These plans differ a great deal in terms of premium costs, maximum coverage limits, deductible amounts, and exclusions. Many plans of protection are available within group policies through an employer where the employer may pay a part or all of the premium costs. The consumer should compare and study various health insurance plans before making a purchasing decision. Basically, insurance plans fall into two major categories: those that cover medical expenses and those that guarantee income in case of disability.

Medical Expenses Insurance

Several general types of medical insurance plans that cover various costs of health care are described here.

Hospitalization insurance.
Hospitalization plans help to cover the costs of a hospital stay. These costs may include: room and board, operating room fees, nursing care, laboratory tests, and many other hospital-related charges.

2

Surgical and medical expense insurance. This insurance helps to cover the cost of physicians' fees both in and out of the hospital. Some insurance plans also cover the costs of medicine and prescriptions.

Major medical insurance. Because the basic health protection plans have maximum coverage limits, major medical insurance is available to protect against losses due to a major or extensive illness or injury. These policies cover the costs that go beyond those covered by the plans already described.

Dental insurance. This is a relatively new type of plan that is rapidly becoming very popular in the United States. "In 1981, it was estimated that about 70 million people had some form of dental insurance" (Gitman and McDaniel, 1983, 456). A dental insurance policy covers part of the costs of dental care.

Disability Insurance

A disability is usually defined as "a condition that prevents you from carrying on your usual occupation" (Greene and Dince, 1983, 141). Because of a disabling sickness or accident, an individual would be prevented from earning an income. Disability insurance makes periodic benefit payments while the person is disabled. Disability insurance is available for both short-term and long-term benefits.

Report 4, continued

Reference List

Enter the list of references line for line as shown at the right. Use single-space mode. DS between the entries.

Make any necessary corrections, then key in the title page as directed below.

Title Page

Enter the information for a title page: report title; your name and your school name; current date. Remember to center each line.

Make any necessary corrections, then store the report on your data disk (if you are using one) as REP4. Print out a copy of the entire report.

Finally, assemble the four pages: title page, two pages of text, and reference list. Staple them across the upper lefthand corner. Your report will then be ready to present to your instructor.

REFERENCES

Gitman, Lawrence J., and Carl McDaniel, Jr. Business World. New York: John Wiley and Sons, 1983.

Greene, Mark R., and Robert T. Dince. Personal Financial Management. Cincinnati: South-Western Publishing Co., 1983.

Hodgetts, Richard M. Personal Financial Management. Reading, MA: Addison-Wesley Publishing Co., Inc., 1983.

Mathur, Ike. Personal Finance. Cincinnati: South-Western Publishing Co., 1984.

WORK EVALUATION

Answer the questions at the right. If any answer is no, check with your instructor to see if you should revise the report and print out a new copy.

Self-Check Questions

	Yes	No
1. Did you place the report title on line 10 from top of page?	—	—
2. Did you leave 3 blank line spaces between the title and the first line of the body?	—	—
3. Did you use DS mode for the body of the report?	—	—
4. Did you DS above and below the side headings?	—	—
5. Did you leave a bottom margin of at least 1 inch on each page?	—	—
6. Are words properly divided at line endings?	—	—
7. Did you number page 2 at the right margin on line 6?	—	—
8. Did you begin the body of page 2 on line 8?	—	—

	Yes	No
9. Did you enter the heading of the reference list on line 10?	—	—
10. Did you SS the items of the reference list?	—	—
11. Did you DS between the entries of the reference list?	—	—
12. Did you begin each reference list entry at the left margin and indent the other lines 5 spaces?	—	—
13. On the title page, did you enter the title on line 16?	—	—
14. Did you enter your name on line 32?	—	—
15. Did you DS between your name and the name of your school?	—	—
16. Did you enter the current date on line 50?	—	—

Key in the report line for line and page for page as shown at the right and on page 34. The report is shown in rough-draft form. As you key the report, you will need to make the corrections indicated. Study the proofreader's marks shown on page 26 before you begin keyboarding so that you will make all corrections properly.

When you have finished the two pages and made any necessary corrections, proceed to page 35 and key in the reference page and the title page.

Computer printers often print copy with distinctive punctuation marks. Study the chart of computer punctuation marks below before you key the copy in Report 5.

	typewriter	computer
ampersand	&	&
comma	,	ˌ
parentheses	( )	{ }
question mark	?	?
quotation marks	''	″
semicolon	;	؛

center the heading → ALTERNATIVE WORK SCHEDULES

In order to improve the work*ing* environment and *to* help increase the productivity and morale of workers, many companies are letting employees adjust their work s*h*cedules. Many employers are trying to move away from the traditional time patterns and are allowing employees to match *their* there work schedules more closely to their lifestyles.

Three of the ~~main~~ modifications in the traditional workday that are being utilized by many org*a*nizations are: the compressed workweek, flexitime, and job sharing.

Compresse*d* Workweek

Typically, the compressed workweek consists of a 4-day, *sp* forty-hour week where the employees work ten hours a day. However, "some organizations are experimenting with a three-day, thirty-six hour week {average of twelve *h*ours per day}" {Quible, 1980, 341}. *a*n advantage of the compressed work week is that workers have an extra day to handle personal matters or partici-pa*t*e in *leisure* ~~fun~~ activities. This additional free time ~~will~~ tend*s* to reduce employee absenteeism and tardiness and to i*n*crease the moral*e* and job satisfaction of the *e*mployees. Another advantage of this schedule is the reduction in the time and *expense* ~~money~~ of commuting to ~~and from~~ work by 20% *sp* each week {Chruden and *#*Sherman, 1984, 42}. One major disadvantage of this work schedule is the employees' increased fatigue *which results from* ~~as an effect of~~ the longer hours worked each day.

Flexitime

Another alternative that is becoming popular is one whereby employees ~~can dictate~~ *may determine* their own daily work schedules. Their arrival and departure times each day are flexib~~a~~*le*~~l~~. However, all employees must work a forty-hour workweek and be ~~there~~ *present* during certain core or peak workload hours each day. Again, absentee-ism and tardiness are reduced under this system. Job satisfac-tion seems to increase because *E*mployees have control over their hours. People can choose to work during their *most* ~~peak~~ productive hours and avoid the traffic congestion at peak commuting times. Not all ~~companies~~ *organizations* are suited to ~~such~~ flexible hours, however*, and* some companies report communication ~~gaps~~ *problems* between ~~the~~ employees as a result of the varied work schedules.

Job Sharing

In Job Sharing, "one permanent, full-time job is shared by *(2)* people who generally split their working hours, job respon-sibilities, and employee benefits" {Keeling and Kallaus, 1983, 260}. This split can be on a daily, weekly, or mont*h*ly basis. Job sharing allows many people to work who are not able *or* ~~to~~ do not wish to work full time. It offers people an opportunity to enjoy more leisure time ~~but~~ *while* still earn*ing* some ~~extra~~ income. Some employers complain that there is an increase in coordinating and record-keeping when there are two employees sharing a job; but (generally) it is felt that the increase in the productivity and morale outweighs any disadvantage.

Report 5, continued

Reference List

Process a reference list for the report using the information shown in rough-draft form at the right. Key the copy line for line. Use single-space mode.

After you enter the data and make any necessary corrections, key in the title page as directed below.

Title Page

Enter the information for a title page: report title; your name and your school name; current date. Remember to center each line.

Make any necessary corrections, then store the report on your data disk (if you are using one) as REP5. Print out a copy of the entire report.

Finally, assemble the four pages: title page, two pages of text, and reference list. Staple them across the upper lefthand corner. Your report will then be ready to present to your instructor.

[References] all caps

Chruden, Herbert J., and Arthur W. Sherman, Jr. Managing Human Resources. 7th Ed. Cincinnati: South-Western Publishing Co., 1984.

Kelling, B. Lewis, and Norman F. Kallaus. Administrative Office Management. 8th ed. cincinnati: South-Western Publishing Co., 1938.

Quible, Zane K. Introduction to Administrative Management. 2d ed. Cambridge, MA: Winthrop Publishers, Inc., 1980. SS

WORK EVALUATION

Answer the questions at the right. If any answer is no, check with your instructor to see if you should revise the report and print out a new copy.

Self-Check Questions

	Yes	No
1. Did you place the report title on line 10 from top of page?	—	—
2. Did you use DS mode for the body of the report?	—	—
3. Are words properly divided at line endings?	—	—
4. Did you number page 2 at the right margin on line 6?	—	—
5. Did you begin the body of page 2 on line 8?	—	—

	Yes	No
6. Did you enter the heading of the reference list on line 10?	—	—
7. Did you SS the items of the reference list?	—	—
8. Are all book titles in the reference list underlined?	—	—
9. Did you begin each reference list entry at the left margin and indent the other lines 5 spaces?	—	—
10. On the title page, did you enter the title on line 16?	—	—

PART 3

WORD PROCESSOR SIMULATION: UNBOUND REPORTS

There are three unbound reports on pages 45-52 for you to key using the word processor simulation: Report 6, Report 7, and Report 8. For each report, you will key the body, the references, and the title page.

The reports are presented to you in script and type-written rough-draft form as they would come to you in an office. Refer, when necessary, to the list of proofreader's marks on page 26.

The reports should be proofread, edited, and corrected before you call for a print-out. After you receive the print-out of a report, assemble the pages in proper sequence and staple all pages as directed.

Using the Word Processor Simulation

In many ways, the word processor simulation is similar to the typewriter simulation. You create a document using a set of commands, and you use a Functions Menu that is identical to the one in the typewriter simulation. However, there are several fundamental differences between the way a typewriter and a word processor work. These differences are reflected in the two simulations:

(1) With a word processor, the printed version of the document may look different from the screen version. In this word processor simulation, the screen version of all documents has a line length of 60 characters and the lines are single-spaced. However, when you print the document, you may select different margins and different line spacing for the printed version of the document.

(2) With a word processor, you do not enter a carriage return at the end of a line. Text continues from one line to the next automatically. You enter carriage returns only when you want to start a new line of text at a specific point—for instance, at the beginning of a paragraph.

(3) With a word processor, you have available several editing commands that allow you to perform functions such as inserting and deleting text.

Processing Text

There are three different modes that are used for processing text in the word processor simulation: Entry mode, Cursor Movement mode, and Delete mode. The mode you are in is always indicated at the bottom of the screen.

Entering text. You will use Entry mode to key text in the document and to insert text at a later time. When you begin creating a document, you will be in Entry mode automatically, and your screen will look like the following display.

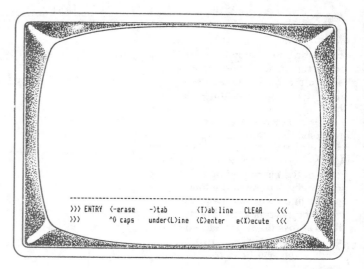

```
>>> ENTRY  <-erase   ->tab      <T>ab line   CLEAR   <<<
>>>        ^O caps   under<L>ine <C>enter   e<X>ecute <<<
```

The bottom two lines of the screen provide a summary of the commands that are available to you in this mode.

- *Keying text.* Whenever you are in Entry mode, you can key text in the document by striking keys for the appropriate characters. It is not necessary to strike a carriage return key at the end of a line. The text continues from one line to the next as you key. Because the document may be reformatted when you print it, you should not hyphenate words at the end of a line (except when copying line for line, as in the reference page).

- *Entering carriage returns.* Enter a carriage return only if you want to start a new line at a specific point. For instance, you should start a new line at the beginning of a paragraph, or when entering a report heading. When you want to start a new line, strike RETURN/ENTER. A carriage return symbol (>) will appear on the screen at the end of the line of text, and the cursor will move to the beginning of the next line. The carriage return symbols will not appear on the printed documents.

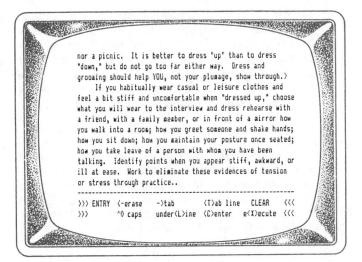

Carriage returns also are used to enter blank lines. With single spacing, enter one carriage return for each blank line. With double spacing, enter one carriage return for every two blank lines.

For example, if you are creating a single-spaced document with one blank line between paragraphs, you should enter two carriage returns at the end of a paragraph—one to end the line of text and another to leave a blank line. For a double-spaced document with only one blank line between paragraphs, you should enter only one carriage return at the end of a paragraph. When you select double-spacing, a blank line will be printed after each line of text automatically.

- *Scrolling.* When the text you have entered reaches the bottom of the screen, it will begin scrolling upward with each carriage return you enter. If you want to view or edit any of the text that has scrolled off the screen, you can retrieve it by using commands in Cursor Movement mode. (This will be explained in a later section.)

- *Erase (←).* You can erase a character or characters you have just keyed by using the ← key. Each time you strike this key, the cursor will move back one space and the previous character will be erased.

- *Caps lock.* As in the other simulations, you can turn the caps lock on or off with the following command:

> Apple, IBM, or TRS-80 Model 4:
> depress the Caps Lock key.
> TRS-80 Model III: hold down the Shift key and strike 0 (zero).

This will allow you to type text in capital letters without having to hold down the Shift key.

- *Tab line <T>.* You can set or clear tabs at any time while in Entry mode by striking Control-T to access the tab line. The tab line will replace the bottom two lines of the screen, as in the following display.

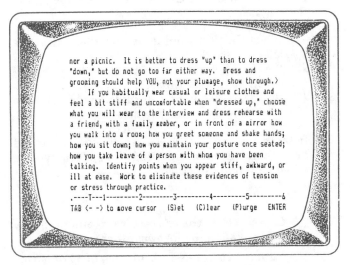

Since you do not set margins until printing the document, the tab line always begins at position 1 and ends at position 60. Each digit in the tab line represents ten spaces: The "1" indicates position 10, the "2" indicates position 20, and so on. If, for instance, you want to set a tab to indent paragraphs five positions, you should set the tab at position 6.

Use the following procedures to set, clear, and purge tabs:

(1) To set a tab, use the → and ← keys to move the cursor to the appropriate position and strike "s."
(2) To clear a tab, use the → and ← keys to move the cursor to the tab you want to clear and strike "c."
(3) To purge all tabs, strike "p" with the cursor at any position.

When you have finished setting or clearing tabs, strike RETURN/ENTER, and the previous bottom two lines of your screen will reappear.

- *Tab key.* Use the tab key (TAB on the Apple microcomputer, → on the TRS-80, and the Tab key on the IBM) to move to each tab stop on a line. If the tab key is used after the cursor is beyond the last tab stop, the cursor will not move.

Underline <L>. You can underline text the same way as you did in the other simulations. Strike Control-L to enter slashes in the spaces before and after words (see pages 11, 12, and 13 for examples).

Remember, there are three cases in which there will not be a space before or after the text to enter a slash:

(1) When the first word to be underlined is at the left margin.
(2) When the first word to be underlined is preceded by a parenthesis.
(3) When the last word to be underlined is followed by punctuation or a parenthesis.

In these cases, enter the slashes directly before and after the appropriate text and the spacing will be taken care of automatically.

Center <C>. You can center text automatically in this simulation, by following these procedures:

(1) With the cursor at the beginning of a line, strike Control-C. A centering symbol (~) will appear on the screen.
(2) Key the text to be centered.
(3) Strike RETURN/ENTER. A carriage return will appear and the cursor will move to the next line.

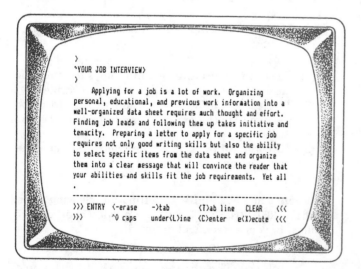

The text will not appear centered on the screen. However, when you print the document, the text will be centered within the margins.

Cancel entry. It is possible to cancel (erase) text that you have keyed by striking ESC on the Apple or IBM computer or CLEAR on the TRS-80 microcomputer. This procedure will cancel all text that you have keyed while in Entry mode. You will be prompted to confirm this request, in order to protect your text in case you strike this key accidentally.

Execute. Whenever you finish entering text or when you want to go into another mode, you must execute your entry by striking Control-X. Your text will remain on the screen, but the command line at the bottom of the screen will change to indicate that you are in Cursor Movement mode.

Editing text. You will use Cursor Movement mode to view or edit text. Whenever you are in Cursor Movement mode, there will be a command summary at the bottom of your screen indicating the available commands in this mode.

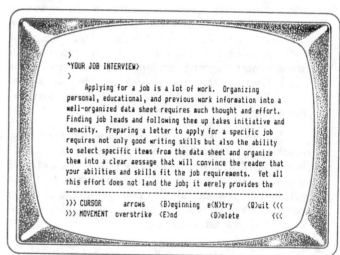

Arrow keys. The four arrow keys (→ ← ↑ ↓) allow you to move the cursor right, left, up, and down. The → and ← keys move the cursor letter-by-letter through the line and then to the next or previous line. The ↑ and ↓ keys move the cursor line-by-line up or down. As you move the cursor up or down, the screen will scroll, several lines at a time, to let you see previous or later text.

Beginning of document <B>. To move the cursor from any place in the document to the beginning, strike Control-B.

- *End of document <E>.* To move the cursor from any place in the document to the end, strike Control-E.

- *Overstrike.* If you want to replace a character or change a word to another one of the same length, follow these procedures for overstriking:

  (1) In Cursor Movement mode, move the cursor so that it is over the first character you want to replace.
  (2) Key the correct character or word. (If you make an error while overstriking, move the cursor to the error and overstrike again.)

You can overstrike all characters, including blanks. However, you cannot overstrike carriage return symbols or centering symbols. (This protects you against accidentally reformatting the document.)

- *Quit <Q>.* When you have finished creating your document, strike Control-Q while in Cursor Movement mode to "quit." The Word Processor Functions Menu will appear on the screen and you will be able to save and/or print your document.

Inserting text. If you make a mistake or want to add text to your document at a later time, you can make an insertion using Cursor Movement and Entry modes. Follow the procedures below:

  (1) In Cursor Movement mode, move the cursor to the position where the first character is to be inserted.
  (2) Strike Control-N to go into Entry mode. The text following the cursor will be temporarily cleared from the screen.
  (3) Key the text to be inserted.
  (4) Strike Control-X to execute the insertion. The text following the cursor will reappear, and you will be back in Cursor Movement mode.

Deleting text. You can delete text from your document by using Cursor Movement and Delete modes.

  (1) In Cursor Movement mode, move the cursor so that it is over the first character to be deleted.
  (2) Strike Control-D to go into Delete mode.
  (3) Strike the space bar until each character to be deleted is covered by an inverse block. (If you accidentally strike the space bar too many times, you can recover the text by striking the ← key. You can also cancel the deletion entirely by striking ESC/CLEAR.)
  (4) Strike Control-X to execute the deletion. The text following the deletion will reformat to close the space left by the deletion.

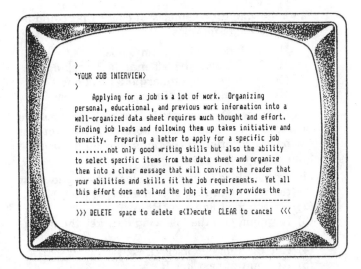

Embedded formatting codes. In the word processor simulation, it is possible to embed formatting codes in the document that affect the way the document will appear when it is printed. These codes can be used to issue the following commands: (1) change margins, (2) change line spacing, (3) eject page, (4) insert blank lines, and (5) suppress page numbers. You can insert these codes in your document while you are keying text in Entry mode. The codes are not included on the Entry command line (because of space limitations), so you should refer to this section in the User's Guide when you want to use these codes.

To embed any of the formatting codes in your document, follow the procedures below:

  (1) At the beginning of a new line, key the code (either capital or lowercase).
  (2) Strike RETURN/ENTER, so that the code is on a line by itself.

When the document is printed, the entire line is removed, so that neither the code nor a blank line will appear.

- *Change margins.* You set margins for your document at the time of printing. If you do not want your margins to be the same for the entire document, you should embed a formatting code to change them at the appropriate places. The code for changing margins consists of the following four characters:

  (1) *
  (2) L or R (for left or right margin)
  (3) + or − (to increase or decrease the margin setting)
  (4) number (indicating the number of positions to increase or decrease the margin setting)

The following are examples of codes that could be used to change margins:

*L+5   Indent left margin 5 positions
*L−3   Outdent the left margin 3 positions
*R−5   Indent right margin 5 positions
*R+3   Outdent right margin 3 positions

For instance, if you want to indent both margins five positions for an extended quotation, then outdent them to their original positions, you should use the following procedures.

(1) At the place in your document where you want to indent margins, key on a line by itself *L+5.
(2) On the next line key *R−5.
(3) Beginning on the following line, key the quotation.
(4) Key on a line by itself *L−5.
(5) Key on the next line R+5.

- *Change spacing.* You set the line spacing for your document (single or double spacing) at the time of printing. (The document appears on the screen in single spacing.) If you want the line spacing to change in your document, use an embedded line spacing code to override the setting for line spacing. There are two embedded spacing codes:

*S1   Change to single spacing
*S2   Change to double spacing

For example, if you want the first part of your document to be double-spaced and the last part to be single-spaced, follow these procedures:

(1) When you reach the part of your document to be single-spaced, key on a line by itself *S1.
(2) When you print the document, set the line spacing for double spacing.

- *Eject page.* When you print your document, you set the "page length." This determines the last line on which text will be printed on each page. For instance, if you set your page length at 60, text will print through line 60 on each page, and the next line of text will begin on a new page. However, if you want a page to end before line 60 (such as the reference page), you need to eject the page after the last line of copy on the page. Embed the code *E at this point. The text following this code will begin printing on a new page.

- *Insert blank lines.* Ordinarily you enter blank lines in your document by keying carriage returns. However, if you want to enter a number of blank lines in your document (for instance in the title page of a report), you should embed a formatting code. (This procedure saves space in your documents, which allows you to key more text in a document and save more documents.) The following code is used to embed blank lines:

*B followed by the number of blank lines

For example to insert five blank lines, use the code *B5. Whether the document is to be single-spaced or double-spaced, the embedded code indicates the actual number of blank lines to insert in your document.

You may need to insert blank lines at the top of a page. When you print a document, you set the "top line" for the document. The top line determines where on each page the first line will print. For instance, for an unbound report, set the top line at 8. This means that the first line of copy on each page (other than the page number) will print on line 8. However, for page 1 you want the first line of text to print on line 10. Therefore, at the beginning of the first page enter the code *B2 to indicate that two blank lines should be inserted before text is printed. (You could enter a carriage return instead. When you print the document in double-spacing, two blank lines will be left.)

- *Suppress page numbers.* When you print a document, you indicate whether or not you want to have page numbers printed on the document. If you choose to have page numbers printed, the first page of your document will not be numbered, but other pages will be numbered consecutively, beginning at page 2. If you want to turn off page numbering at a particular point in your document, embed the code *P on the appropriate page and all following pages will not have page numbers.

For example, you want the body of a report but not the references and title page to have page numbers. You should use the following procedures:

(1) Key the body of the report.
(2) Embed the eject page code (*E).
(3) Embed the suppress page numbers code (*P).
(4) Key the references and title page.
(5) When printing the document, choose to have page numbers printed.

Your report will be printed with page numbers for the body of the report, but without page numbers for the references and title page.

Determining Print Settings

In the word processor simulation, you determine print settings for your document at the time of printing. When you select the option from the Word Processing Functions Menu to print your document, you receive a screen that looks like the following display:

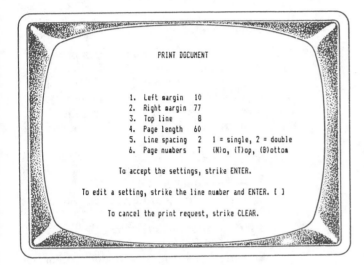

You key the following settings at this screen:

(1) *Left margin*. The left margin refers to the number of spaces at the left of the page. For a left margin of one inch or 10 pica spaces, you should set the left margin at 10. The left margin must be 3 or greater.

(2) *Right margin*. The right margin refers to the last position in which text will be printed. There are 85 pica characters on a page. Therefore, for a right margin of exactly one inch, you would key a right margin setting of 75. However, in order to obtain a more uniform right margin, it is recommended that you set the right margin at 77 for a margin of approximately one inch.

The right margin must be set at 82 or less. The right margin minus the left margin must be at least 20.

(3) *Top line*. The top line refers to the first line of the paper on which text will be printed. If you want the first line of text to appear on line 8, for example, you should key a top line setting of 8.

If you print your document without page numbers or with page numbers at the bottom (see below), the top line must be at least 1. If you print your document with page numbers at the top, the top line must be at least 7.

(4) *Page length*. The page length refers to the last line of a page on which text will be printed. There are 66 lines of text on a page, with six lines to an inch. Therefore, if you want a bottom margin of one inch (six lines), you should set the page length at 60.

If you print your document without page numbers or with page numbers at the top, your page length must be 66 or less. If you print your document with page numbers at the bottom, the page length must be 61 or less.

(5) *Line spacing*. The line spacing refers to the number of lines indicated by each carriage return in the document. You can set the line spacing at 1 for single spacing or 2 for double spacing.

(6) *Page numbers*. You can key one of three entries for the page numbers setting:

N: This indicates that you do not want page numbers printed on your document.

T: This indicates that you want page numbers printed at the top of the page, on line 6 at the right margin. This numbering method is used in unbound and leftbound reports.

B: This indicates that you want page numbers printed at the bottom of the page, on line 62 in the center. This numbering method is used in topbound reports.

If you choose to have page numbers printed, the pages will be numbered consecutively, beginning with page 2.

Completing a Word Processor Assignment

Selecting the assignment. Each time you begin an assignment with the word processor simulation, follow these procedures:

(1) Sign on to the computer using Disk 1 for Module A (see page 3).

(2) At the Main Menu, key the number 3 and strike RETURN/ENTER for the word processor simulation.

(3) At the Word Processor Functions Menu, key 1 and strike RETURN/ENTER for the function Create or Edit Document.

Keying the exercise. Use the following procedures to key a report.

(1) Access the tab line and set a tab at 6 (for indenting paragraphs and reference page entries). (See page 37.)

---

(2) Enter a carriage return. (When you print the document in double spacing, two blank lines will be added to the top margin of 8, so the heading will print on line 10.)

(3) Key the body of the report, using the tab key to indent and the centering command to center the report title.

(4) Embed the eject page code (*E).

(5) Embed the code *S1 to change to single spacing.

(6) Embed the code *P to suppress page numbers.

(7) Enter a carriage return so the Reference page title will begin on line 10.

(8) Key the reference page line for line. In order to indent a line in the references, you must enter a carriage return at the end of the previous line. For each source listed in the references, follow these procedures:

   (a) Key the first line of the copy. Enter a carriage return.

   (b) Use the tab key to indent, then key the next line and enter a carriage return.

   (c) Repeat b for every following line.

Note concerning underlining. If underlined text continues from one line to the next, you should enter slashes (using Control-L) to begin and end the underlining on *both* lines. If an indented line begins with underlined text, remember to backspace one position to enter the slash.

(9) At the end of the references, embed the eject page code (*E).

(10) Enter eight carriage returns or embed the code *B8. (When you set your top line at 8, this code will add another 8 lines and the first line of text on the title page will print on line 16.)

(11) Key the report title, using the centering command.

(12) Enter 15 carriage returns or embed the code *B15. (You are inserting 15 blank lines in order to enter the name of the writer on the sixteenth line below the report title.)

(13) Center the name of the writer.

(14) Enter an extra carriage return to leave a blank line.

(15) Center the name of the school.

(16) Enter 15 carriage returns or embed the code *B15.

(17) Center the date.

(18) Return to Cursor Movement mode by striking Control-X.

(19) Strike Control-Q to quit.

Using the document management functions. After you finish keying your document, follow these procedures:

(1) *Save the document.* If you are using a data disk, save the document by selecting function 3 and following the directions on the screen. If you are not using a data disk, go on to step 2.

(2) *Print the document.*

• *Preparing to print.* If you have a printer attached to your computer, make sure your printer is properly prepared. If you are using a printer attached to another computer, follow these procedures to prepare for printing.

   (a) Exit to the title screen and remove the disks.

   (b) Take the disks to a computer with a printer attached and insert the Report Formatting disk.

   (c) Proceed to the Word Processor Functions Menu.

   (d) Retrieve the document by selecting function 4 and following the directions on the screen. You will not see the document but you will receive a message telling you that the document is being retrieved.

   (e) Make sure the printer is properly prepared.

• *Printing.* Follow these procedures to print the document.

   (a) Select function 2 Print Current Document from the Word Processor Functions Menu.

   (b) At the next screen, titled "Print Document," enter these print settings for the document.

Left margin	10
Right margin	77
Top line	8
Page length	60
Line spacing	2
Page numbers	T

   (c) At the following screen accept the settings, if correct, or edit the settings, if you made a mistake. The document will print, followed by a document identification page with your name, the date, and the name of your document (if you saved it).

   (d) If you want to save the print settings (so that you do not have to enter them before printing the document again), save the document again, using the same document name as before.

Other functions. As in the typewriter simulation, there are four functions on the Word Processor Functions Menu that you may use occasionally: Retrieve a Document from Data Disk, Catalog Data Disk, Erase a Document from Data Disk, and Clear Current Document.

- *Retrieve a Document from Data Disk.* You can retrieve a document that you have saved on your data disk by selecting function 4 from the Word Processor Functions Menu. Once you have cleared a document from the computer's memory, you must retrieve it from your data disk before you can view, edit, or print it.

- *Catalog Data Disk.* You may catalog the data disk by selecting function 5 from the Word Processor Functions Menu. Just as in the other simulations, this function will provide you with a list of the names of all documents stored on the data disk.

- *Erase a Document from Data Disk.* You may erase a document that you created previously in any of the simulations by selecting function 6 and following the directions on the screen. Use this function if your data disk becomes full or if you want to remove documents that you no longer want on the data disk.

- *Clear Current Document.* If you have created or retrieved a document, you must clear the document from the computer's memory before you can create or retrieve another document. For instance, if you create, save, and print a document, you must clear the document from the computer's memory before you can create another. If you retrieve, edit, and save a document, you also must clear that document before retrieving or creating another. To clear a document, select function 7 and follow the directions on the screen. In order to protect the document in case you selected function 7 accidentally, you will be prompted to confirm this selection.

Finishing an Assignment in Another Session

You may start an assignment in one session and finish it in another with the word processor simulation. To do so, follow these procedures if you have a data disk:

(1) When you want to stop keying the document, strike Control-X for Cursor Movement mode, then strike Control-Q to return to the Word Processor Functions Menu.
(2) Save the document on the data disk.
(3) Exit to the title screen and power down the computer.
(4) At the next session, proceed to the Word Processor Functions Menu.
(5) Retrieve the document from the data disk.

(6) Select function 1 to continue the document.
(7) You will be in Cursor Movement mode automatically. Use Control-E to move to the end of your document.
(8) Strike Control-N to go into Entry mode and continue keying text.

If you would like to finish an assignment in another session but do not have a data disk on which to store your document, follow these procedures:

(1) When you want to stop keying the document, strike Control-X then Control-Q to return to the Word Processor Functions Menu. Key to the end of the report body or to the end of a page before you end the session.
(2) Print the document.
(3) Exit to the title screen and power down the computer.
(4) At the next session, proceed to the Word Processor Functions Menu.
(5) Select Function 1 to create a document.
(6) Begin keying at the point where you left off, at the beginning of a page.

Beginning Another Assignment

After you complete an assignment, you may want to start another. If so, follow these procedures:

(1) At the Word Processor Functions Menu, select function 7 to clear the current document, then follow the directions on the screen.
(2) After the document has been cleared, select function 1 Create or Edit Document.
(3) Follow the same procedures as before to create the new document.

Editing a Document

You may edit any Word Processor document that you have saved on the data disk by following these procedures:

(1) Retrieve the document from the data disk.
(2) Select function 1 to edit the document.
(3) Edit the document using the commands available in the word processor simulation.
(4) Strike Control-Q to return to the Word Processor Functions Menu.
(5) Save the revised document. Use the same name as you did for the first version, and the revised document will replace the earlier version on the data disk.
(6) Print the revised document, if desired. If you did not save the print settings, you must specify them again. If you saved the print settings, you may edit or accept the previous settings.

FUNCTIONS OF MANAGEMENT

Before beginning the following
report formatting assignments,
be sure you have studied the
material on pages 36-43 so that
you will know how to use your
computer in preparing Reports
6, 7, and 8.

Report 6

Key in the report shown at the
right and on page 46. In the
word processor simulation the
"word wrap" feature is in operation; therefore, do not strike the
RETURN key at line endings
except at the end of a paragraph
or heading. The "word wrap"
feature will determine the line
endings when the report is
printed.

You are responsible for centering, placement, and spacing
decisions.

When you have finished the
two pages, make any necessary
corrections. Then proceed to
page 46 and key in the reference
page and the title page.

REVISIONS

After you have printed the report, make the following revision:

Following the first paragraph (¶)
of the report, insert the additional introductory ¶ shown
below.

¶ The management process
encompasses four important
functions: planning, organizing,
directing, and controlling.

Print out a copy of the revised
report.

The management of any organization is a process which involves making the best use of all available resources in order to meet specific goals. Irrespective of the size, type, or nature of the organization, the effectiveness of its management group determines whether the organization succeeds.

Planning

Planning involves anticipating the future and determining both where the organization wants to be at some point in that future and what it wants to accomplish. Such planning is implemented by the establishment of objectives. Objectives or goals are defined as "specific, hoped-for results that can be expressed in quantitative and measurable terms with timetables set for achievement" (Gitman and McDaniel, 1983, 104). Once the objectives have been developed, management can then design procedures and policies for meeting the objectives.

Organizing

Next, the management team must organize the organization's resources so that the objectives can be met. Here management goes through a process of deciding what must be done, how it will be done, and who can best do it in order to accomplish with greatest efficiency what the organization has set out to do. Management must decide what activities and procedures will be performed, establish a division of labor, and structure people and activities in order to produce an effective, efficient workflow.

Reference List

Enter the list of references shown at lower right line for line, making the corrections indicated. Enter a carriage return at the end of each line. Use SS mode; DS between entries.

When you finish entering the data, make any necessary corrections, then key in the title page.

Title Page

Prepare a title page: report title, your name and your school name; current date.

Make any necessary corrections, then store the report on your data disk (if you are using one) as REP6. Print out a copy of the entire report.

Assemble all report pages and staple them in the upper lefthand corner.

WORK EVALUATION

Answer the questions below. If any answer is no, make the needed corrections, print out a revised copy, and reassemble the report.

Self-Check Questions

	Yes	No
1. Did you place the report title on line 10 from top of page?	—	—
2. Did you number page 2 at the right margin on line 6?	—	—
3. Did you begin the body of page 2 on line 8?	—	—
4. Did you enter the heading of the reference list on line 10?	—	—
5. On the title page, did you enter the title on line 16?	—	—
6. Did you identify and correct all errors before printing out a copy of the report?	—	—

2

Directing

Directing includes those management activities that "encourage subordinates to work toward the achievement of the company's goals" (Cunningham, Aldag, and Swift, 1984, 130). The directing process involves leading, motivating, and communicating.

Controlling

In carrying out the controlling function, management "measures current performance against expected outcomes and takes necessary action to reach goals" (Steade, Lowry, and Glos, 1984, 97). In order to insure that the actual performance is in harmony with intended performance, management must set performance standards, establish a system for measuring current performance, and take corrective action if standards are not being met.

References

Cunningham, William H., Ramon J. Aldag, and Christopher M. Swift. Introduction to Business. Cincinnati: South-Western Publishing Co., 1984.

Gitman, Lawrence J., and Carl McDaniel, Jr. Business World. New York: John Wiley and Sons, 1983.

Steade, Richard D., James Lowry, and Raymond Glos. Business: Its Nature and Environment, An Introduction. Cincinnati: South-Western Publishing Co., 1984.

Key in the report shown at the right and on page 48, using word processor simulation. As you key, make the corrections indicated.

When you have finished the two pages, make needed corrections. Then proceed to page 49 and key in the reference page and the title page.

EMPLOYMENT INTERVIEWS

The employment interview plays a very important *role* ~~roll~~ in the employee selection process. After ~~closely~~ studying the applicant's data sheet and application form, the interviewer *conducts* ~~holds~~ an interview to discover more about the applicant's skills, qualifications, and inter*e*st in the job. ~~Then~~ the interviewer is able to make ~~certain~~ judgments regarding the applicant's appearance, poise, and personality. The interviewer has the responsibility for matching the right person with the right job. Bec*a*use the interview process is *so* ~~pretty~~ important in selecting the best employee for the job, ~~many~~ organizations "are realizing the necessity for using adequately trained interviewers" {Quible, 1980, 225}.

There are *several* ~~seven~~ types of interviews. The types differ in the amount of control or structure that is *exercised* ~~used~~ by the person who conducts the interview. ~~In addition,~~ they *also* differ "according to the methods that are used to obtain information and to elicit attitudes and feelings from an applicant" {Chruden and Sherman, 1984, 135}. Of all the ~~various~~ types of interviews, three are most common: patterned, direct, and indirect.

Patterned Interview

The patterned interview is a highly stru*c*tured type in which the interviewer asks each *applicant* ~~person~~ a standard list of questions and records the responses on a form. This type of interview is useful when there are many applicants for the same job. Because *the* answers to the s*o*me questions *are* ~~have been~~

2

recorded for all ap~p~licants, no information is overlooked and the applicants' responses can later be ~analyzed~ *compared*. The ~list of~ questions ~is~ *are* standardized; there fore, time can be saved because more than one interviewer can ~hold~ *conduct* interviews at the same time for the same job.

Direct Interview

The direct interview is ~somewhat~ less structured. The interviewer asks the applicant direct questions about his or her background and qualifications for the ~p~*a*rticular job. The questions asked require *concise* ~short, pithy~ answers; however, the interviewer must ask questions that require answers other than yes or no. Otherwise, the interviewer may not get enough information from the *applicant* ~interviewee~. This type of interview does result in helpful information *about* ~concerning~ the applicant's qualifications for the ~particular~ job, but it does *not* get much information about the ~aspirant's views~ *applicant's attitudes*, feelings, and so fou~r~th.

Indirect Interview

The indirect or unstructured interview is "based upon the idea that more can be learned about applicants by stimulating them to talk about themselves than by asking them ~lots of~ direct questions" {keeling and Kallaus, 1983, 87}. An applicant has a good de~a~l of control in this type of interview because the i~n~terviewer asks open-ended questions which ~will~ allow the applicant to talk more freely. The indirect interview takes more time than the other types and requires an interviewer who can listen, refrain from ~barging in~ *interrupting*, but still keep the interview on target.

REVISIONS

After you have printed the report, make the following revision:

Make the last sentence in ¶ 2 a ¶ by itself: insert a carriage return after the previous sentence, and indent.

Print out a copy of the revised report.

Report 7, continued

Reference List

Enter the list of references shown at the right line for line. Enter a carriage return at the end of each line. Use SS mode; DS between entries.

When you finish entering the data, make any necessary corrections, then key in the title page.

Title Page

Enter the information for a title page: report title; your name and your school name; current date.

Make any necessary corrections, then store the report on your data disk (if you are using one) as REP7. Print out a copy of the entire report.

Assemble all report pages and staple them in the upper lefthand corner.

REFERENCES

Chruden, Herbert J., and Arthur H. Sherman, Jr. Managing Human Resources. 7th ed. Cincinnati: South-Western Publishing Co., 1984.

Keeling, B. Lewis, and Norman F. Kallaus. Administrative Office Management. 8th ed. Cincinnati: South-Western Publishing Co., 1983.

Quible, Zane K. Introduction to Administrative Office Management. 2d ed. Cambridge, MA: Winthrop Publishers, Inc., 1980.

WORK EVALUATION

Answer the questions at the right. If any answer is no, make the needed corrections, print out a revised copy, and reassemble the report.

Self-Check Questions

Yes No

1. Did you place the report title on line 10 from top of page? ___ ___
2. Did you DS above and below side headings? ___ ___
3. Did you leave a bottom margin of at least 1 inch on each page? ___ ___
4. Did you number page 2 at the right margin on line 6? ___ ___
5. Did you begin the body of page 2 on line 8? ___ ___

Yes No

6. Are left and right margins approximately equal in width? ___ ___
7. Did you enter the heading of the reference list on line 10? ___ ___
8. Are all book titles in the reference list underlined? ___ ___
9. On the title page, did you enter the title on line 16? ___ ___
10. Did you identify and correct all errors before printing out a copy of the report? ___ ___

Key in the report shown at the right and on pages 51-52, using word processor simulation. As you key, make the corrections indicated.

When you have finished the three pages, make needed corrections. Then proceed to page 52 and key in the reference page and the title page.

Center title — Credit

The use of credit has become an ~~important~~ integral part of the way of American life. The increase in volume of consumer credit available to americans has had a very positive affect upon the volume of retail sales in the United States.

Credit has ~~often~~ been defined as the "present use of future income" {Martin, Petty, and Klock, 1982, 148}. Under any type of credit agreement, you are promising to use your future tomorrow's income to pay for products or services that you are using or enjoying today. You are also usually required to pay a charge for the privilege of postponing payment for these goods or services, that you are using or enjoying today.

The buy now, pay later system is a very useful method for the consumer to use in managing personal finances. It is ~~very~~ important to recognize, however, the various disadvantages as well as the advantages of using credit.

Advantages of credit

Convenience and emergency use. Many consumers choose to use credit cards rather than carry ~~big~~ large sums of cash. They charge goods or services throughout the month and pay only once when the bill is recieved. This system provides a record of expenses which many consumers find helpful. Also, credit may come in very handy during financial emergencies. If the consumer is short of cash when an emergency arises, credit may be a temporary solution to the problem.

Immediate use of Goods and Protection from Inflation.
Rather than saving the money to purchase high-cost items, many
consumers choose to use credit to purchase these ~~items~~ goods.   They
have the use of the goods while paying for them overtime.
Because of inflation, the price of a product may rise while
the consumer is saving to purchase that product.   The use of
Credit lets the ~~person~~ consumer buy the product at a lower price.

Disadvantages of Credit

Danger of misuse.   It is very easy to buy more than you
can afford to pay for.   Financial Experts estimate that 5
percent of ~~all~~ Americans are in serious financial trouble
(Hodgets, 1983, 114).   Much of this trouble is ~~because of~~ due to the
misuse of credit.   Marketing and advertising tactics of ~~many~~
retailers often contribute to the misuse of credit.   ~~Their~~
delayed-payment offers and telephone purchases using credit
card numbers are among the tactics used to get people to buy
on impulse; that is, before they have time to ~~access~~ assess the total
of other payments that must be made at that later time.

A ~~good~~ rule of thumb to go by is that "no more than 20%
of any family's take-home earnings should go toward meeting
credit payments" (Mathur, 1984, 192).   Many people forget to
consider the once-a-year payments for such things as life
insurance, automobile insurance, and tax payments that may be
coincident with payments for credit purchases.

High cost of credit.   The cost of credit can become very
high.   Before singing any kind of agreement for credit, it is
essential that the consumer know how much that credit is going

3

to cost. Credit cost is ~~figured~~ *measured* by the annual percentage
rate or APR. A common APR for credit card perchases and
installment purchases in 18 percent, but the rate can vary.
Comparison of credit costs proves that a ~~s~~consumer is ~~smart~~ *wise to*
shop around for credit. *In some cases,* ~~Sometimes~~ a secured bank loan ~~proves~~
may ~~to~~ be less expensive than an installment purchase through a
retail store.

Reference List
Enter the list of references shown at the right line for line. Enter a carriage return at the end of each line. Use SS mode; DS between entries.

When you finish entering the data, make any necessary corrections, then key in the title page.

Title Page
Enter the information for a title page.

Make any necessary corrections, then store the report on your data disk (if you are using one) as REP8. Print out a copy of the entire report. Assemble all report pages and staple them in the upper left-hand corner.

REFERENCES

Hodgetts, Richard M. <u>Personal Financial Management</u>.
    Reading, MA: Addison-Wesley Publishing Company, Inc.,
    1983.

Mathin, John D., William Petty, and David R. Klock. <u>Per-
    sonal Financial Management</u>. New York: McGraw-Hill,
    Inc., 1982.

Mathur, Ike. <u>Personal Finance</u>. Cincinnati: South-Western
    Publishing Co., 1984.

WORK EVALUATION
Answer the questions at the right. If any answer is no, make the needed corrections, print out a revised copy, and reassemble the report.

Self-Check Questions

	Yes	No
1. Did you place the report title on line 10 from top of page?	—	—
2. Did you DS above and below the side headings?	—	—
3. Did you underline paragraph headings and end them with a period?	—	—

	Yes	No
4. Did you number pages 2 and 3 at the right margin on line 6?	—	—
5. Did you enter the heading of the reference list on line 10?	—	—
6. Did you identify and correct all errors before printing out a copy of the report?	—	—

MODULE B:
LEFTBOUND REPORTS

LEFTBOUND REPORTS:
Formatting Guides

Binding

As the word "leftbound" suggests, leftbound reports are bound along the left edge. Special report covers (clasp, comb, or ring binders) are used for this purpose. Short reports, such as the ones in this module, are often stapled at three equally spaced points along the left edge, about a half inch in from the left edge of the paper.

Margins

Top margin. The top margin of a leftbound report is the same as that of an unbound report: On page 1 the main heading is placed on line 10 for 10-pitch machines and on line 12 for 12-pitch machines.

On page 2 and following pages, the page number is placed on line 6 at the right margin, and the text continues on line 8.

Side margins. To provide the space needed for binding at the left, a 1½-inch left margin is used for leftbound reports. This is 15 pica or 10-pitch spaces; 18 elite or 12-pitch spaces. A 1-inch right margin is used, as for unbound reports.

Bottom margin. A bottom margin of at least 1 inch (6 line spaces) is used for leftbound reports, as for unbound ones.

Pagination

The first page of a leftbound report is usually not numbered. On page 2 and following pages, the page number is placed on line 6 at the right margin.

Reference List

The heading REFERENCES is placed on line 10 for 10-pitch machines and on line 12 for 12-pitch machines—the same placement as the main heading on page 1. A 1½-inch left margin and a 1-inch right margin are used. A QS (quadruple space) is left between the heading and the first entry. Individual entries are single-spaced (SS); a double space (DS) is left between entries.

Title (Cover) Page

The title of the report is placed on line 16 (8 double spaces in double-space mode) and is centered over the *line of writing*; that is, the title is centered between the left and right margin settings.

> To determine the horizontal center point for leftbound reports:
> 1. Add the margin-set figures for the left and right margins (from the line-of-writing or format-line scale).
> 2. Divide the total by 2; note the resulting figure, the center point for leftbound reports.
> 3. Use this figure as the point from which to backspace when centering any item horizontally in leftbound format.

The name of the writer and school (or business) affiliation begin on line 32 (16 lines below the title). The date is placed on line 50 (16 lines below the authorship information).

All lines of the title page are centered horizontally over the *line of writing*.

See models on pages 55 and 56.

PART 1

COMPUTER-FORMATTED LEFTBOUND REPORTS

Reports 9 and 10 on pages 57-62 are to be keyed and formatted in leftbound style, as computer-formatted exercises. Key these reports as four assignments: Report 9A, Report 9B, Report 10A, and Report 10B. Follow the procedures "Completing a Computer-Formatted Exercise" on pages 12-15. Notice that the margins have been pre-set at 15 and 75 for these leftbound reports. A tab has been preset at 45 to indicate the center.

You will use Disk 2 for the Module B and Module C reports.

Start heading or title on line 10.

Line 10 → SERENDIPITY

Leave 3 blank line spaces.

1½"

Have you ever gone to the dictionary to look up a word and discovered the meaning of a new word which caught your eye on the same page? Have you ever turned to a certain volume in a set of encyclopedia to read about a specific topic only to discover information pertaining to a new and interesting subject about which you knew nothing before you opened the volume? For that matter, have you ever searched in a book shop for a book you wanted to read and been attracted by the titles and covers of other books that you found exciting or even irresistible?

If you have ever experienced these or similar incidents, you should be able to understand the meaning of the word "serendipity." The word was coined by Horace Walpole from the Persian fairy tale The Three Princes of Serendip in which the princes made fortunate discoveries by accident. Modern dictionaries define serendipity as the faculty of making fortunate and unexpected discoveries by accident.

DS

Some of the greatest discoveries in the world have come about as the result of the process of serendipity. Alert scientists and other well-known scholars, bent on studying one particular set of phenomena, have uncovered new facts which have opened up broad fields for further exploration. You can be certain that the process of serendipity is at work as we probe into outer space, look into the depths of

1"

At least 1" or 6 lines

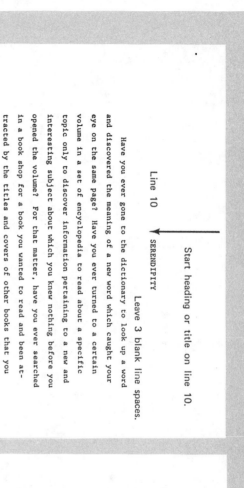

Enter page number on line 6.

2

DS

1½"

the oceans, search beneath the outer crust of the earth, or explore the behavior of a new vaccine.

DS

Although most of us are not destined to become well-known scientists or scholars, serendipity can propel us beyond what is self-evident and into the realm of discovery. To use serendipity to our advantage, though, we must develop two important related traits: curiosity and imagination.

DS

Curiosity

DS

"Curiosity is one of the permanent and certain characteristics of a vigorous mind" (Johnson, 1751, 1). A curious person is one who is eager to acquire information or knowledge. Not content with a single convenient source of facts or ideas, the curious person searches for other sources of relevant information to extend readily available knowledge. Without a curious attitude, one is not likely to experience serendipity often.

DS

Imagination

DS

One of the definitions of imagination is "the act of creating new images or ideas by combining previous experiences." Doing so helps us to deal with new facts, ideas, and experiences in novel and creative ways. Those who use imagination well often create new knowledge. As the poet Keats (1817, 2) once said: "The imagination may be compared to Adam's dream--he awoke and found it truth."

DS

Curiosity often precedes serendipity; applied imagination often follows it. This cause-act-effect relationship helps to make learning by discovery an exciting experience.

1"

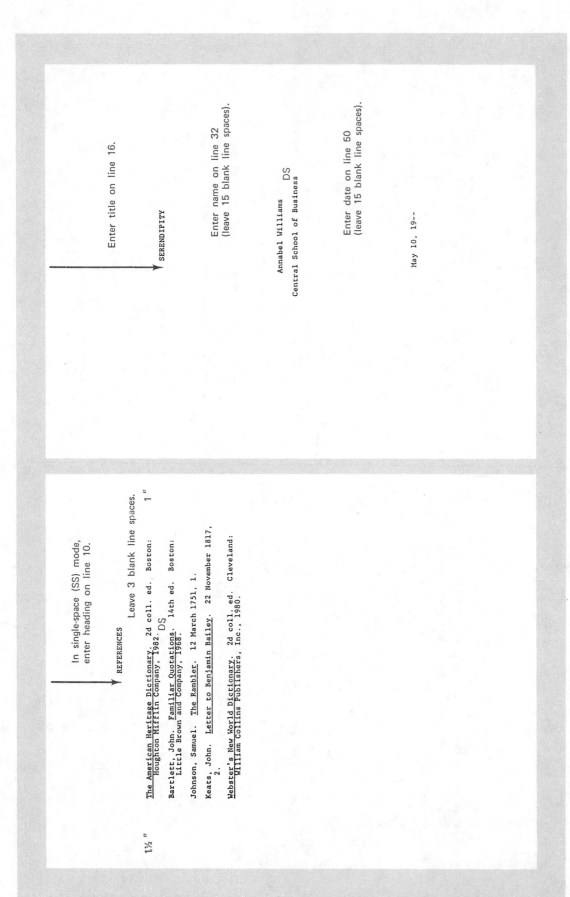

1½"

In single-space (SS) mode, enter heading on line 10.

Leave 3 blank line spaces.   1"

REFERENCES DS

The American Heritage Dictionary, 2d coll. ed. Boston: Houghton Mifflin Company, 1982.

Bartlett, John. Familiar Quotations. 14th ed. Boston: Little Brown and Company, 1968.

Johnson, Samuel. The Rambler. 12 March 1751, 1.

Keats, John. Letter to Benjamin Bailey. 22 November 1817, 2.

Webster's New World Dictionary. 2d coll. ed. Cleveland: William Collins Publishers, Inc., 1980.

Enter title on line 16.

SERENDIPITY

Enter name on line 32 (leave 15 blank line spaces).

Annabel Williams DS
Central School of Business

Enter date on line 50 (leave 15 blank line spaces).

May 10, 19--

Title Page of Leftbound Report

List of References for Leftbound Report

Before beginning the report
formatting assignments, be
sure you have studied the material on pages 54-56, including
the illustrations of a leftbound
report.

Report 9A

Key in the report shown at the
right and on page 58. Wait for
each prompt to appear on the
display screen telling you what
you are to do next. Enter the
copy line for line and page for
page as shown.

When you have finished,
store the report on your data
disk (if you are using one) as
REP9A.

Print out a copy of your
work.

You will prepare a reference
page and a title page to complete the report.

Note that the main heading is
centered over the *line of writing*; that is, it is centered in the
space between the left and right
margin settings.

SERENDIPITY

Have you ever gone to the dictionary to look up a word
and discovered the meaning of a new word which caught your
eye on the same page? Have you ever turned to a certain
volume in a set of encyclopedia to read about a specific
topic only to discover information pertaining to a new and
interesting subject about which you knew nothing before you
opened the volume? For that matter, have you ever searched
in a book shop for a book you wanted to read and been attracted by the titles and covers of other books that you
found exciting or even irresistible?

If you have ever experienced these or similar incidents, you should be able to understand the meaning of the
word "serendipity." The word was coined by Horace Walpole
from the Persian fairy tale The Three Princes of Serendip
in which the princes made fortunate discoveries by accident.
Modern dictionaries define serendipity as the faculty of
making fortunate and unexpected discoveries by accident.

Some of the greatest discoveries in the world have come
about as the result of the process of serendipity. Alert
scientists and other well-known scholars, bent on studying
one particular set of phenomena, have uncovered new facts
which have opened up broad fields for further exploration.
You can be certain that the process of serendipity is at
work as we probe into outer space, look into the depths of

the oceans, search beneath the outer crust of the earth, or explore the behavior of a new vaccine.

Although most of us are not destined to become well-known scientists or scholars, serendipity can propel us beyond what is self-evident and into the realm of discovery. To use serendipity to our advantage, though, we must develop two important related traits: curiosity and imagination.

Curiosity

"Curiosity is one of the permanent and certain characteristics of a vigorous mind" (Johnson, 1751, 1). A curious person is one who is eager to acquire information or knowledge. Not content with a single convenient source of facts or ideas, the curious person searches for other sources of relevant information to extend readily available knowledge. Without a curious attitude, one is not likely to experience serendipity often.

Imagination

One of the definitions of imagination is "the act of creating new images or ideas by combining previous experiences." Doing so helps us to deal with new facts, ideas, and experiences in novel and creative ways. Those who use imagination well often create new knowledge. As the poet Keats (1817, 2) once said: "The imagination may be compared to Adam's dream--he awoke and found it truth."

Curiosity often precedes serendipity; applied imagination often follows it. This cause-act-effect relationship helps to make learning by discovery an exciting experience.

Report 9B

Reference List

Process a reference list for the report using the information shown on index cards at the right. Key the copy line for line as shown. Be sure to put the entries in alphabetical order. Use single-space mode. DS between the entries. The reference list will be a separate page at the end of the report.

Next, enter the title page as directed below.

Note that the heading REFER-ENCES is centered over the *line of writing*.

Bartlett, John. *Familiar Quotations*. 14th ed. Boston: Little Brown and Company, 1968.

Webster's New World Dictionary. 2d coll. ed. Cleveland: William Collins Publishers, Inc., 1980.

The American Heritage Dictionary. 2d coll. ed. Boston: Houghton Mifflin Company, 1982.

Keats, John. *Letter to Benjamin Bailey*. 22 November 1817, 2.

Johnson, Samuel. *The Rambler*. 12 March 1751, 1.

Title Page

Enter the information for a title page as the computer prompts you, part by part. Note that your name, school name, and date are centered over the line of writing.

When you are finished, store the reference list and title page on your data disk as REP9B.

Print out a copy of your work.

Finally, assemble the four pages: title page, two pages of text, and reference list. Staple them at three equally spaced points along the left margin. Your report will then be ready to present to your instructor.

Information for the title page

TITLE:	**SERENDIPITY**
NAME:	Your own
SCHOOL:	Your own
DATE:	Current

Report 10A

Enter the copy shown at the right and on page 61 as two pages of a leftbound report. Wait for each prompt to appear on the display screen telling you what you are to do next. Enter the copy line for line and page for page as shown.

   When you have finished, store the report on your data disk as REP10A.

   Print out a copy of your work.

   You will prepare a reference page and title page to complete the report.

OFFICE SOUND CONTROL

The sound level in offices has a definite effect on the productivity of office workers. Most companies recognize this fact and have taken steps to control the unwanted noise that is caused by people and equipment. The objective of sound control is to produce an office environment that is conducive to workers' physical and psychological well-being.

Sound control also results in a more efficient work environment. Research has proven that "workers in a noisy environment require almost 20 percent more time to complete a given amount of work than do those in a quiet place" (Ruprecht and Wagoner, 1984, 373).

Sound is measured in decibels. A decibel is the smallest sound detectable by the human ear. The suggested maximum noise level for the average office is in the range of 40-60 decibels (Keeling and Kallaus, 1983, 341). There are two major steps to achieving a healthy sound environment. First, the sources of noise must be identified, and then proper measures can be taken to control noise in the office.

Sources of Noise

The two major sources of office noise are equipment and people. The automated equipment that has been introduced in today's offices can be very noisy. Word processors, typewriters, computers, printers, copiers, and telephones all contribute to raising the noise level in the office. Office personnel create noise with their discussions, conferences, and conversations regarding their work assignments. Also, the movement of workers as they carry out their work assignments creates office noise.

Controlling Noise

Once the sources of office noise have been identified, measures can be taken to control this noise to some degree. These measures include eliminating whatever noise can be eliminated and absorbing as much residual noise as possible.

Eliminating noise. It may be necessary to change the layout of the office so as to eliminate some of the unwanted noise. By doing this, it is possible to relocate the noisy equipment to areas where people will not be disturbed. It is also possible to reassign workers to areas where they will be working more closely with those personnel who have similar work assignments. Doing this tends to confine to more segregated areas the conversation and movement required by certain similar work assignments.

Absorbing noise. Any noise control effort has to be based on the fact that "hard surfaces reflect sounds while soft surfaces absorb them" (Keeling and Kallaus, 1983, 342). Therefore, sound-absorbing materials should be used wherever possible. Such materials include floor coverings, ceilings, draperies, and wall coverings. Sound-absorbing devices such as padding, covers, and shields can be installed on or under equipment to absorb excessive noise.

Report 10B

Reference List

Process a reference list for the report using the information shown on index cards at the right. Key the copy line for line as shown. Be sure to put the entries in alphabetical order. Use single-space mode. DS between the entries. The reference list will be a separate page at the end of the report.

Next, enter the title page as directed below.

Keeling, B. Lewis, and Norman Kallaus. *Administrative Office Management*. 8th ed. Cincinnati: South-Western Publishing Co., 1983.

Ruprecht, Mary M., and Kathleen P. Wagoner. *Managing Office Automation*. New York: John Wiley & Sons, Inc., 1984.

Title Page

Enter the information for a title page as the computer prompts you, part by part. Note that each line is centered over the line of writing.

When you are finished, store the reference list and title page on your data disk as REP10B.

Print out a copy of your work.

Finally, assemble the four pages: title page, two pages of text, and reference list. Staple them at three equally spaced points along the left margin.

Information for the title page

TITLE: **OFFICE SOUND CONTROL**

NAME: **Your own**

SCHOOL: **Your own**

DATE: **Current**

PART 2
TYPEWRITER SIMULATION: LEFTBOUND REPORTS

There are three reports on pages 64-72: Report 11, Report 12, and Report 13. Key these reports in leftbound style using the typewriter simulation. Using Disk 2, follow the procedures in the section "Selecting the Assignment" on page 24. Use the following procedures for keying each assignment:

(1) Select format settings for your document (see page 22). For leftbound reports use the following settings:

Left margin:	15
Right margin:	75
Line spacing:	2

(2) Using the procedures for the typewriter simulation, roll the paper in (page 23).

(3) Set tabs (page 23). For leftbound reports, set tabs at 21 and 45.
(4) Key the first page of the report and eject the page.
(5) Key the second page of the report and eject the page.
(6) Access the format screen by striking Control-F and change the line spacing to "1" for single spacing.
(7) Key the references and eject the page.
(8) Key the title page.
(9) Strike Control-Q when finished. You will return to the Typewriter Functions Menu.

Complete each assignment, following the procedures in the section "Using the Document Management Functions," beginning on page 24.

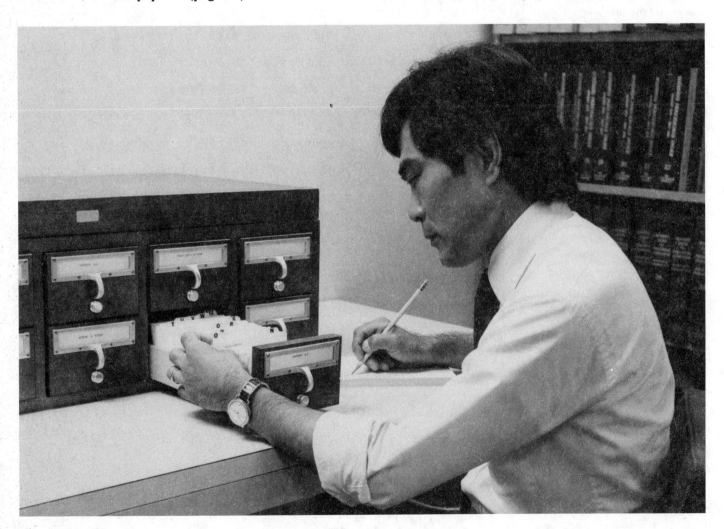

Before beginning the report formatting assignments, study the material on page 63 which provides the procedures for using your computer as a type-writer.

Report 11

Key in the report shown at the right and on page 65. The copy is presented in typed and rough-draft form. Enter it line for line and page for page as given, making the corrections indicated.

Make any necessary cor-rections, then proceed to page 66 and key in the reference page and the title page.

QWERTY VS. DVORAK

The first practical American typewriter was patented in 1868 by Sholes, Glidden, and Soule. It was manufactured and sold by Remington & Sons in 1874. The location of keys on the Remington typewriter soon became the standard arrange-ment for keyboards of nearly all other makes. With minor changes and additions, this standard or QWERTY keyboard is almost the same as that of the millions of typewriters used in homes, schools, and business and government offices even today (Bliven, 1954, 114).

Keyboard reform--efforts to make the typewriter key-board more efficient and easier to operate--has a very long history. Hammond, for example, in 1881 marketed a machine with an "improved" keyboard. Hoke in 1924 was issued a pa-tent for a keyboard arranged according to frequency of use of the letters and facility of the various fingers. Dvorak and Dealey in 1932 received a patent for still another key-board arrangement which they called a "Simplified" keyboard (Robinson, 1975, 2). Not one of these attempts to improve the arrangement of the letters received more than temporary interest.

From time to time, a new spark of interest in simplify-ing the QWERTY keyboard is ignited, flames for a while, then dies. This may turn out to be true today regarding the cur-rent interest in the Dvorak-Dealey keyboard, now referred to

as the Dvorak simplified keyboard. It is believed by many
that the Hoke and the Dvorak keyboards are more scientific
in ~~layout~~ design than the standard or Qwerty keyboard and should be
more efficient to ~~run~~ operate. Just how much more efficient one ~~type~~
or the other is remains a ~~mute~~ moot question, nevertheless. Many
claims are made, but there is little proof that is based on
valid, reliable research (Erickson, 1982, 311-316).

In 1956, Strong reported on the ~~base~~ basis of his research
data that to retrain a typist skilled on the standard keyboard to use a "Simplified" keyboard with equal facility required ~~around~~ about one hundred hours! Moreover, he reported that
"traditional" typists outgained "simplified" typists during
a ~~time~~ period of further training to improve skill. He concluded
that "adoption of the Simplified keyboard for use by the
Federal Government cannot be justified based on the findings
of this experiment" (Strong, 1956, 41).

For many years, cost of converting keyboards from the
QWERTY to the Dvorak ~~system~~ arrangement dissuaded schools and businesses from making the change. Now that ~~the~~ conversion is as
simple as ~~hitting~~ pressing a key and using a template, at least on
some computers, the choice rests on the comparative efficiency of operation (MacDonald, 1984, 31). Unfortunately,
"Simplified" keyboard ~~components~~ proponents have not provided comparative data on which to make a sound decision. Until valid
and reliable data are available, the current interest in the
Dvorak keyboard ~~will~~ is likely to remain in the ~~hands~~ heads of a ~~fairly~~ limited group of Dvorak devotees (Neill, 1980, 671-673).

Report 11, continued

Reference List

Enter the list of references line for line as shown at the right. Use single-space mode. DS between the entries. The reference list will be a separate page at the end of the report.

Make any necessary corrections, then key in the title page as directed below.

NOTE: Center the heading REFERENCES over the *line of writing*.

Title Page

Enter the information for a title page. Center each line over the *line of writing*.

Make any necessary corrections, then store the report on your data disk as REP11. Print out a copy of the entire report.

Finally, assemble the four pages: title page, two pages of text, and reference list. Staple them at three equally spaced points along the left margin (about a half inch in from the left edge).

REFERENCES

Bliven, Bruce. The Wonderful Writing Machine. New York: Random House, 1954.

erickson, Lawrence W.   The Dvorak Simplified versus the Standard Keyboard." The Balance Sheet, April 1982, 311-16.

McDonald, Stephen. "Dvorak Typewriter Keyboard May At Last Have Chance to Challenge Qwerty Design." Wall Street Journal, 21 June 1984, 31.

Neill, Shirley Boss. "Dvorak vs. Qwerty: Will Tradition Win Again?" Phi Delta Kappan, June 1980, 671-73.

Robinson, Jerry W. "An Idea Whose Time Has Come . . . Again?" Century 21 Reporter, Spring 1975, 2.

Strong, Earle P. A Comparative Experiment in Simplified Keyboard Retraining. Washington, DC: General Services Administration, 1965.

WORK EVALUATION

Answer the questions at the right. If any answer is no, make the needed corrections, print out a revised copy, and reassemble the report.

Self-Check Questions

	Yes	No
1. Did you place the report title on line 10 from top of page?	—	—
2. Did you center the title over the line of writing?	—	—
3. Did you leave a 1½ inch left margin and a 1 inch right margin?	—	—
4. Did you leave a bottom margin of at least 1 inch on each page?	—	—

	Yes	No
5. Did you number page 2 at the right margin on line 6?	—	—
6. Did you begin the body of page 2 on line 8?	—	—
7. Did you enter the heading of the reference list on line 10?	—	—
8. On the title page, did you center each line over the line of writing?	—	—

Key in the report shown at the right and on page 68. The copy is presented in handwritten and rough-draft form, but you will enter it line for line and page for page as given.

Make any necessary corrections, then proceed to page 69 and key in the reference page and the title page.

NOTE: Center the main heading over the *line of writing*.

FUNCTIONS OF MONEY ⟩ *Center main heading*

Money is essential to any economic system. Generally, money is considered to be any ~~media~~ *medium* that is acceptable as payment for goods and services and for the discharge of debt {Auerback, 1982, 8}. In order for money to be considered as acceptable for use within a society, it must perform certain functions. It must serve a medium of exchange, a standard of value, and a store of value.

Side heading ⎡ Medium of exchange ⎤ ¶ ~~A Type~~ *To serve as a medium* of exchange is the *basic* function of money. It is used to buy and sell goods and services in a monetary economic system. Society has advanced to the use of money as a system of exchange; early trade was based upon an intricate system ~~of~~ (barter) which depended ~~on~~ *upon* the trade of goods or services for other goods or services. This barter system depended upon what is ~~called~~ *known as* a "double coincidence of wants" {Kamerschen, 1984, 5}; that is, ~~somebody~~ *a person* with goods to exchange needed to find another person who not only desired to purchase these *specific* goods but also has *d* ~~certain~~ goods to offer in exchange that were desired by the other person. Finding (2) *sp.* people with this "double coincidence of wants" and goods to exchange became inefficient and time-consuming. Money as a medium of exchange permits us to ~~trade our~~ *exchange* goods for money and then exchange that money for goods we desire.
~~to buy.~~ ¶

2

Standard of Value

Money becomes the yardstick by which the worth [value] of all goods and services are [is] measured. We call these money values prices and measure everything bought and sold in terms of money value. Because prices are quoted in [terms of] dollars and cents (or whatever other label a society places upon its money values), standardized economic arithmetic and accounting become possible within the monetary system.

Store of value

The store-of-value function of money permits people to store or accumulate wealth. It also allows them to postpone the purchase of good[s] and services. If this time option was [were] not available, people would need to buy desired goods and services immediately upon being paid for their labor or sale of goods and services. Because money serves as a store of value, it is possible either for people to put some money aside for future needs or to pay for goods over a period of time. These options are possible because the value of money is standardized and is relatively stable over a period of time within the Economic System.

Report 12, continued

Reference List

Process a reference list for the report using the information shown on index cards at the right. Key the copy line for line. Be sure to put the entries in alphabetical order. Use single-space mode. DS between the entries.

Make any necessary corrections, then key in the title page as directed below.

NOTE: Center the heading REFERENCES over the *line of writing.*

Auerbach, Robert D. *Money, Banking, and Financial Markets.* New York: Macmillan Publishing Co., Inc., 1982.

Kamerschen, David R. *Money and Banking.* 8th ed. Cincinnati: South-Western Publishing Co., 1984.

Hailstones, Thomas J. *Basic Economics.* 7th ed. Cincinnati: South-Western Publishing Co., 1984.

Title Page

Enter the information for a title page. Center each line over the *line of writing.*

Make any necessary corrections, then store the report on your data disk as REP12. Print out a copy of the entire report.

Finally, assemble the four pages in proper sequence and staple them at three equally spaced points along the left margin (about a half inch in from the left edge).

WORK EVALUATION

Answer the questions at the right. If any answer is no, make the needed corrections, print out a revised copy, and reassemble the report.

Self-Check Questions

	Yes	No
1. Did you place the report title on line 10 from top of page?	—	—
2. Did you DS above and below the side headings?	—	—
3. Did you leave a bottom margin of at least 1 inch on each page?	—	—
4. Did you leave a 1½ inch left margin and a 1 inch right margin?	—	—
5. Did you number page 2 at the right margin on line 6?	—	—
6. Did you begin the body of page 2 on line 8?	—	—

	Yes	No
7. Did you enter the heading of the reference list on line 10?	—	—
8. Did you SS the items of the reference list?	—	—
9. Did you begin each reference list entry at the left margin and indent the other lines 5 spaces?	—	—
10. Did you center the information on the title page over the line of writing?	—	—

Key in the report shown at the right and on page 71. The copy is presented in rough-draft form, but you will enter it line for line and page for page as shown, making the marked corrections.

After you key in the report, make any necessary corrections, then proceed to page 72 and key in the reference page and the title page.

NOTE: Center the main heading over the *line of writing*.

Center main heading [TEMPORARY WORKERS IN TODAY'S OFFICES

Temporary office help service*s* place office workers in office assignments for ~~short~~ *limited* periods of time. The client company pays a fee to the temporary help service for ~~using~~ *the use of* these temporary employees.

The [office temporary] help industry is growing rapidly. Currently, temporary services bill client companies "about $2.5 billion a year and employ 3.5 million workers" {Farkas, 1983, 78}. the industry has "grown at an annual rate of about ~~twenty~~ *20* percent in the last few years and its business doubles every 3.5 years" {Naisbitt, 1982, 236}.

The indu*s*try stresses to the client companies two advantages of using temporary *office* help: lower labor ~~expenditures~~ *costs* and a constant resource of trained, skilled workers.

Lower Labor Costs

Because the temporary service ~~takes over~~ *assumes* many *of the* personnel functions, labor costs of the client companies are reduced sign*i*ficantly. The temporary service has the task of [interviewing, recruiting, training, and paying the employees. They also handle the employees' bonding, tax and Social Security deductions, and medical insurance. Client companies also lower their labor costs for [things] such [as "record-keeping costs, payroll taxes, worker's compensation, vacation and sick time, and usge of the employees only when needed" {Keeling and Kallaus, 1983, 83}. Employee benefit costs are borne by the temporary service thereby reducing

farther the client companies' labor costs. Because client

companies hire these workers only during the peak work load

periods, they do not have to pay them except for theperiods

worked. Because "75 percent of all Business expenses are

personnel-related" {Farkas, 1983, 80}, temporary services

maintain their customers can cut down on their labor costs

by utilizing temporary employees.

Resource of Train, Skilled Woerkers

Several of the large, nationwide temporary office hlep

services are becoming active in training their new workers.

They are constantly striving to match the worker's talents

and skills with customers' demands.

The temporary help services are experiencing greatest

growth in the area of data processing. Consequently, the

training that is being offered is primarily in this area in

order to meet demands for employers to work in today's auto-

mated offices on atemporary basis.

Varying approaches are being used for this training by

several leading firms in the industry. Though self-paced

hands-on, and simulated training, the temporary employees

are trained and cross-trained until they are experienced in

the various aspects of word processing and are ready to step

into ofices of client companys as qualified and productive

employees.

Reference List

Process a reference list for the report using the information shown on index cards at the right. Key the copy line for line. Be sure to put the entries in alphabetical order. Use single-space mode. DS between the entries.

Make any necessary corrections, then key in the title page as directed below.

NOTE: Center the heading REFERENCES over the *line of writing*.

Title Page

Enter the information for a title page. Center each line over the *line of writing*.

Make needed corrections, then store the report on your data disk as REP13. Print out a copy of the entire report.

Finally, assemble the four pages in proper sequence and staple them at three equally spaced points along the left margin (about a half inch in from the left edge).

Naisbitt, John. Megatrends. New York: Warner Books, Inc., 1982.

Farkas, David. "Temporary Services Sing a New Song." Modern Office Procedures, May 1983, 78-82.

Keeling, B. Lewis, and Norman F. Kallaus. Administrative Office Management. 8th ed. Cincinnati: South-Western Publishing Co., 1983.

WORK EVALUATION

Answer the questions at the right. If any answer is no, make the needed corrections, print out a revised copy, and reassemble the report.

Self-Check Questions

	Yes	No
1. Did you use DS mode for the body of the report?	—	—
2. Did you DS above and below the side headings?	—	—
3. Are words properly divided at line endings?	—	—
4. Did you leave a 1½ inch left margin and a 1 inch right margin?	—	—
5. Did you center the report title and the reference heading over the line of writing?	—	—

	Yes	No
6. Did you SS the items of the reference list?	—	—
7. Did you DS between the entries of the reference list?	—	—
8. Are all book and magazine titles in the reference list underlined?	—	—
9. On the title page, did you enter the title on line 16?	—	—
10. Did you center the information on the title page over the line of writing?	—	—

PART 3
WORD PROCESSOR SIMULATION: LEFTBOUND REPORTS

Use the word processor simulation to key Reports 14, 15, and 16 in leftbound style.

Using Disk 2, follow the procedure "Completing a Word Processor Assignment" on pages 41-43, except use the following print settings for leftbound reports:

Left margin:	15
Right margin:	75
Top line:	8
Page length:	60
Line spacing:	2
Page numbers:	T

Before beginning the report formatting assignments, study the material on page 73 which provides the procedures for using your computer as a word processor.

Report 14

Key in the report shown at the right and on page 75. The copy is presented in script form. Enter the copy continuously rather than line for line; the "word wrap" feature of the word processor will determine the line endings when the report is printed.

Make any needed corrections, then proceed to page 76 and key in the reference page and the title page.

NONVERBAL COMMUNICATION

Nonverbal communication refers to all of the ways that we communicate with others without the use of words. These unspoken or nonverbal messages may accompany our verbal messages; they may substitute for verbal messages; and they add a great deal of information to our verbal messages.

Research has shown that in most communications, people communicate approximately 10 percent of their message by the words they use, 30 percent by their tone of voice, and 60 percent by their nonverbal communications (Cooper, 1981, 147). It is essential for everyone to be aware of nonverbal communication so that we may communicate our messages more successfully and also interpret the messages of others with more accuracy.

Many categories of nonverbal communications may be conveyed through the various senses. The majority of our nonverbal messages, however, are conveyed visually by our appearance and body movements.

Appearance

People form an impression of us based upon how we look. This includes our clothes and accessories, our hair and how it is styled, and our personal grooming. People tend to interpret our appearance as evidence of our personal values, attitudes, and beliefs (Wolf and Kuiper, 1984, 133). Our appearance says a lot about how we feel about ourselves (our self-image) and how we feel about others. The "dress for success" and "wardrobe engineering" concepts are based upon studies showing how a person's appearance influences the reactions and feelings of others.

Body Movements

Our body movements include such things as our posture, the way we walk and sit, our gestures, our eye movements, and our facial expressions. All these aspects of our bodily behavior give clues to our attitudes and feelings. The way we position our bodies and the way we use our hands convey a great deal about our unspoken thoughts. But perhaps the very best indicators of how we really feel about a situation or another person are our facial expressions and the contact we have with that person with our eyes. Eye contact and facial expressions convey many personal messages about us, influence how others will react to us, and have a big effect upon the success of our communications.

What we wear and how we look can have a dramatic impact on our success in the world of business -- from the initial job interview to the rate at which we climb our career ladders (Michulka, 1983, 149).

REVISIONS

BEFORE YOU PRINT A COPY OF THE REPORT, make the following change given to you by the originator of the report:

Insert the sentence given at the right at the end of the ¶ about Appearance (just before the ¶ about Body Movements). Then proceed to page 76, key in the reference page and title page, and print out a copy of the report.

Report 14, continued

Reference List

Process a reference list for the report using the information shown on index cards at the right. Key the copy line for line and enter a carriage return at the end of each line. Be sure to put the entries in alphabetical order. Use SS mode; DS between the entries.

When all errors have been corrected, key in the title page as directed below.

Title Page

Enter the information for a title page: report title; your name and your school name; current date.

When all errors have been corrected, store the report on your data disk as REP14. Print out a copy of the entire report.

Finally, assemble all pages in the proper sequence and staple them at three equally spaced points along the left margin (about a half inch in from the left edge).

Michulka, J. H. *Let's Talk Business.* 2d ed. Cincinnati: South-Western Publishing Co., 1983.

Cooper, Ken. "Nonverbal Communication and Business." *Effective Communication on the Job.* 3d ed. New York: AMACOM, A Division of American Management Association, 1981.

Wolf, M. P., and Shirley Kuiper. *Effective Communication in Business.* 8th ed. Cincinnati: South-Western Publishing Co., 1984.

WORK EVALUATION

Answer the questions at the right. If any answer is no, make the needed corrections, print out a revised copy, and reassemble the report.

Self-Check Questions

	Yes	No
1. Did you place the report title on line 10 from top of page?	—	—
2. Did you leave 3 blank line spaces between the title and the first line of the body?	—	—
3. Did you leave a 1½ inch left margin and a 1 inch right margin?	—	—
4. Did you leave a bottom margin of at least 1 inch on each page?	—	—
5. Did you enter the heading of the reference list on line 10?	—	—
6. Did you SS the items of the reference list?	—	—

	Yes	No
7. Did you begin each reference list entry at the left margin and indent the other lines 5 spaces?	—	—
8. Did you center the information on the title page over the line of writing?	—	—
9. On the title page, did you enter the title on line 16?	—	—
10. Did you identify and correct all errors before printing out a copy of the report?	—	—

Report 15

Key in the report shown at the right and on page 78. The copy is presented in rough-draft and corrected script form. Be sure to make all corrections as indicated. Enter the copy continuously rather than line for line; the "word wrap" feature of the word processor will determine the line endings when the report is printed.

Make any needed corrections, then proceed to page 79 and key in the reference page and the title page.

Computer Ethics

Have you ever copied from another students' paper and thereby taken credit for someone else's work? Have you ever made ~~copies~~ a copy of a cassette tape to avoid having to buy one? Or have you ever made a copy of a friend's video cassette or a rented movie so that you could ~~watch~~ view it again with friends without further cost? If you have done any of these things, you have ~~disobeyed~~ violated the standards of ethical behavior.

"Ethics" refers to the code of morals of ~~some~~ a particular person, group, or profession. Ethical behavior of a group or of an individual falls within the standards of conduct ~~usually~~ considered by society acceptable. Some of these standards may simply be entries in a list of rules of conduct; others have been formalized into laws.

Illegal Uses Of Computers

Newspapers and magazines are ~~full of~~ rife with stories about persons who have beencaught engaging in computer crime (Immel 1984, 65). Some people have ~~changed~~ falsified computer records for their own gain; for example, changing ~~your~~ one's grade in a course. Others have transferred funds from bank accounts of other individuals into their own. Some have had merchandise sent to bogus businesses at no charge and were ~~therefore~~ thus able to sell the goods personally and pocket the Money. And there are those who in anger damaged ~~some~~ computer systems or destroyed data (Clark and Lambrecht, 1985, 14-15).

2

Some Guides for Computer Users

In addition to those acts that can be labeled as _classified_ computer crimes, there are borderline acts the legality of which is still being tested but which are unethical, _at best._

Copyrighted material. Most computer software (disks or cassettes) is copyrighted. Those who _duplicate_ copy programs without permission of the copyright holder are in violation of the copyright law. A copyright notice generally appears on diskette labels, and a full copyright _statement_ appears on one of the early screens of each diskette. Read this _statement_ notice carefully and abide by it. Most software programs are protected to keep the novice programmer from making an unauthorized copy. A more _sophisticated_ intelligent programmer is often able to break the protection but is being unethical in doing so. Ethical code: Do not copy copyrighted material.

Computer spying. Because computers are _often_ shared, in schools and in business, stored information is sometimes accessible to those for whom it is not intended. To protect classified data, businesses have begun to use pass words or other _schemes_ things to limit access to such information (Emmett, 1984, 98). Computer information (data and words) is much like personal mail and should not be spied _upon_ on whether out of curiosity or for personal gain. Ethical code: Use only your own computer files and those _intended_ meant for open access; do not spy on other people's computer mail and records.

REVISIONS

After you have printed the report, make the following revision:

Delete the following two sentences from the ¶ about copyrighted material:

Most software programs are protected to keep the novice programmer from making an unauthorized copy. A more sophisticated programmer is often able to break the protection but is being unethical in doing so.

Then print out a copy of the revised report.

Report 15, continued

Reference List

Process a reference list for the report using the information shown on index cards at the right. Key the copy line for line. Be sure to put the entries in alphabetical order. Use SS mode; DS between the entries.

When all errors have been corrected, key in the title page.

> **NOTE:** An underline at the beginning of a reference citation indicates that the author is the same as in the preceding entry. Type the underline the length of the author's last name (in this listing, 5 spaces) and follow it with a period. If your computer printer cannot print underlines, use hyphens in place of the underline.

Title Page

Enter the information for a title page: report title; your name and your school name; current date.

When all errors have been corrected, store the report on your data disk as REP15. Print out a copy of the entire report.

Finally, assemble all pages in the proper sequence and staple them at three equally spaced points along the left margin (about a half inch in from the left edge).

Immel, A. Richard. "Data Security." *Personal Computing*, May 1984, 65-68.

(Immel)

_____. "Computer Ethics." *Popular Computing*, June 1984, 65-68.

Emmett, Arielle. "Thwarting the Data Thief." *Personal Computing*, January 1984, 98-105, 204-5.

Clark, J. F., and J. J. Lambrecht. *Information Processing: Concepts, Principles, and Procedures.* Cincinnati: South-Western Publishing Co., 1985.

WORK EVALUATION

Answer the questions at the right. If any answer is no, make the needed corrections, print out a revised copy, and reassemble the report.

Self-Check Questions

	Yes	No
1. Did you DS above and below the side headings?	—	—
2. Did you underline paragraph headings and end them with a period?	—	—
3. Did you leave a 1½ inch left margin and a 1 inch right margin?	—	—
4. Did you leave a bottom margin of at least 1 inch?	—	—
5. Did you number page 2 at the right margin on line 6?	—	—
6. Did you begin the body of page 2 on line 8?	—	—

	Yes	No
7. Did you SS the items of the reference list?	—	—
8. Did you underline all book and magazine titles in the reference list?	—	—
9. Did you enclose in quotation marks the titles of magazine articles in the reference list?	—	—
10. Did you identify and correct all errors before printing out a copy of the report?	—	—

Key in the report shown at the right and on page 81. Make corrections as indicated. The "word wrap" feature of your computer will determine the line endings when the report is printed.

After all corrections have been made, proceed to page 82 and key in the reference page and the title page.

NOTE: A quotation of four or more lines is blocked in SS mode 5 spaces in from each side margin. This procedure requires resetting margins and spacing. (See pages 39-40 for how to do this on the computer.)

ELEMENTS OF A VALID CONTRACT

A contract is a legally enforceable agreement between two parties to do or not to do something. In order for the contract to be valid and enforceable in the courts, it must contain certain elements: There must be a mutual agreement between the parties; the parties to the contract must be considered legally competent; there must be an exchange of value or consideration between the parties; the purpose of the contract must be legal; and the contract must be in the proper legal format.

Mutual agreement

Both parties to a contract must understand what they are agreeing to. In order for this mutual agreement to take place, there must be a specific offer and an acceptance.

Offer. The characteristics of an offer are:

{1} the proposal must be definite; {2} the proposal must be made with the intention that the offeror {person making the offer} be bound by it; and {3} the proposal must be communicated by words or actions to the offeree {the one to whom it is made} {Warmke and Wyllie, 1983, 79}.

Acceptance. Within a reasonable period of time, the offeree must communicate specific acceptance of the offer to the offeror.

Competent Parties

The parties to the contract must be considered legally competent; that is, they must be able to understand what they are agreeing to. ^Persons ~~People~~ who are minors, insane, or under the influence of drugs or alcohol (aren't) considered to be ~~legally~~ competent parties.

Consideration

Each party to a contract must agree to give or to give up something of ^value ~~worth~~ in order for required consideration to be present. This something of ^value ~~worth~~ may be ~~their~~ "money, goods, services, or the forbearance {giving up} of a legal right" {Rachman and Mescone, 1982, 524}.

Legal Form

Contracts may be made in ^either oral ~~form~~ or written form; however, certain contracts must be written in order to be valid. Those contracts which must be ^in writing ~~written~~ are those that involve ~~the~~ transfer of personal property worth more than $500, cannot be completed within (1) year, or pertain to the proposed sale of real estate.

REVISIONS
BEFORE YOU PRINT A COPY OF THE REPORT, make the following revision:

Following the ¶ about Consideration, insert the ¶ about Legal Purpose given at the right. Then proceed to page 82, key in the reference page and title page, and print out a copy of the report.

Legal Purpose

A contract cannot be legally enforceable if any action agreed to is against the law. Also, contracts considered to be "contrary to good morals and general public policy are unenforceable" (Harwood, 1983, 141).

Report 16, continued

Reference List

Process a reference list for the report using the information shown on index cards at the right. Key the copy line for line. Be sure to put the entries in alphabetical order. Use SS mode; DS between the entries.

When all errors have been corrected, key in the title page.

Title Page

Enter the information for a title page: report title; your name and your school name; current date.

When all errors have been corrected, store the report on your data disk as REP16. Print out a copy of the entire report.

Finally, assemble all pages in the proper sequence and staple them at three equally spaced points along the left margin (about a half inch in from the left edge).

Rachman, David J., and Michael H. Mescone. *Business Today*. 3d ed. New York: Random House, Inc., 1982.

Harwood, Bruce A. *Real Estate Principles*. 3d ed. Reston, VA: Reston Publishing Company, Inc., 1983.

Warmke, R. F., and E. D. Wyllie. *Consumer Economics*. 10th ed. Cincinnati: South-Western Publishing Co., 1983.

WORK EVALUATION

Answer the questions at the right. If any answer is no, make the needed corrections, print out a revised copy, and reassemble the report.

Self-Check Questions

	Yes	No
1. Did you place the report title on line 10 from top of page?	—	—
2. Did you DS above and below side headings?	—	—
3. Did you underline paragraph headings and end them with a period?	—	—
4. Did you single space the block quotation and indent it 5 spaces from each side margin?	—	—

	Yes	No
5. On the title page, did you enter the title on line 16?	—	—
6. Did you enter your name on line 32?	—	—
7. Did you DS between your name and the name of your school?	—	—
8. Did you enter the current date on line 50?	—	—

MODULE C:
TOPBOUND REPORTS

TOPBOUND REPORTS:
Formatting Guides

Binding

Topbound reports are bound along the top edge. Special report covers (clasp, comb, or ring binders) are used for this purpose. Short reports, such as those in this module, are often stapled at three equally spaced points along the top edge, about a half inch down from the top edge of the paper.

Margins

Top margin. The top margin of a topbound report is about a half inch deeper than that of an unbound report to allow for binding. On page 1 the main heading is placed on line 12 for 10-pitch machines and on line 14 for 12-pitch machines.

On page 2 and following pages, the report text continues on line 10. In topbound reports, the page number is centered at the bottom of the page.

Side margins. Side margins for topbound reports are the same as for unbound ones: 1 inch. That is 10 spaces on 10-pitch machines, 12 spaces on 12-pitch machines.

Bottom margin. A bottom margin of at least 1 inch (6 lines) is used for topbound reports. Page numbers are placed *within* this margin space.

Pagination

The first page of a topbound report is usually not numbered. On page 2 and following pages, the page number is centered on line 62 from the top edge of the page (the 5th line space from the bottom of the page).

Reference List

The heading REFERENCES is centered on line 12 for 10-pitch machines and on line 14 for 12-pitch machines—the same placement as the main heading on page 1. A 1-inch left margin and a 1-inch right margin are used. A QS (quadruple space) is left between the heading and the first entry. Individual entries are single-spaced (SS); a double space (DS) is left between entries.

Title (Cover) Page

The title of the report is centered on line 18 (9 double spaces in double-space mode) from the top edge of the page.

The name of the writer and school (or business) affiliation begin on line 34 (16 lines below the title). The date is placed on line 52 (16 lines below the authorship information).

All lines of the title page are centered horizontally on the page.

Except for the wider top margin and the placement of page numbers at the bottom of the pages, topbound format is identical to unbound format.

See models on pages 85 and 86.

PART 1

TYPEWRITER SIMULATION: TOPBOUND REPORTS

Because the format features of topbound reports are very similar to those of the unbound reports you have already studied, you will not key any computer-formatted topbound reports. Reports 17 and 18 on the following pages will be formatted using the typewriter simulation.

Use the same procedures as for completing an unbound report (see page 24), except for the following:

(1) Insert Disk 2.
(2) Adjust the top margin so that it is appropriate for topbound reports.
(3) Center the page number on line 62.

Start heading or title on line 12.

Line 12

LEARNING TO LISTEN

Leave 3 blank line spaces.

Elementary school children are estimated to spend over half their school day listening. Managers in business spend up to 70 percent of their workday listening. People, in general, spend over 40 percent of their waking time listening. In spite of our obvious dependence upon listening, few people listen well. DS

Hearing and listening are two different but interrelated processes. Hearing is a mechanical activity that is difficult to avoid; listening is a physical and mental process that takes deliberate effort (Smeltzer and Waltman, 1984, 188). In simple terms, you hear with your ears, but you listen with your brain.

Formal attempts to improve listening skills have increased since World War II. These attempts fall into two categories: self-help strategies and directed-training programs.

Self-Help Strategies DS
DS

Special books and parts of general communication books have been written on how to listen effectively. Such materials offer a better understanding of the listening process and give guides to help us practice better listening methods. For example, they say that we must be highly motivated to listen well; that is, we must intend to listen and not merely to hear. They tell us that we must concentrate on what the speaker is saying and to ignore irrelevant distractions. They suggest what to listen for: the main idea, major supporting points, and the message structure.

1"

At least 1" or 6 lines

Page 1 of Topbound Report Manuscript

Enter first line of copy on line 10.

They urge us to organize mentally what is being said and to take notes in outline form. In other words, they tell us how to use the 75 percent time difference between the speed of thinking and the slower speed of speaking. DS

The guides have been helpful to some individuals, but they have not been tested in a formal way to measure actual gains in listening effectiveness. Further, only a small percentage of people have the self-discipline and perseverance to profit from self-help strategies. DS

Directed-Training Programs DS
DS

During the 1960's, several research studies were conducted to determine the effects of a variety of formal training methods on listening ability (for example, Devine, 1961; Edgar, 1961). Using a test-train-retest strategy, such researchers discovered that formal training programs with improvement goals established by a pretest and measured by a posttest provided the motivation to improve listening skills. They also found that specially designed training materials presented according to a prescribed schedule resulted in significant gains in listening effectiveness when compared with listening test results from students who did not undergo the special training. DS

This is not to say that the guides offered by the self-help strategists do not work, for many of the suggestions were incorporated in the training programs. Rather, it says that if the guides are to work, they must be formally structured, practiced, and tested rather than attempted on a self-help basis.

1"

2

Center page number on line 62.

Page 2 of Topbound Report Manuscript

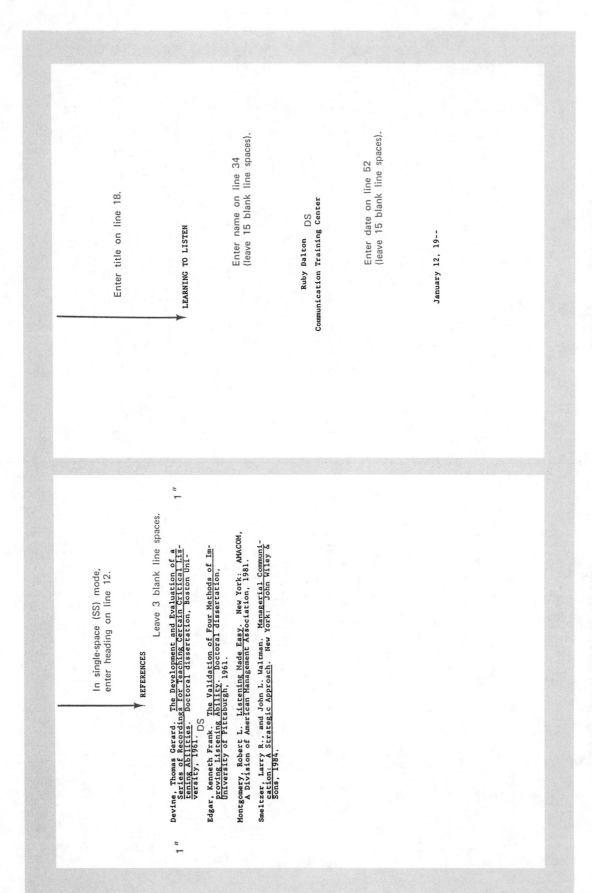

Title Page of Topbound Report

Enter title on line 18.

LEARNING TO LISTEN

Enter name on line 34
(leave 15 blank line spaces).

Ruby Dalton DS
Communication Training Center

Enter date on line 52
(leave 15 blank line spaces).

January 12, 19--

List of References for Topbound Report

In single-space (SS) mode,
enter heading on line 12.

REFERENCES   Leave 3 blank line spaces.

1"

Devine, Thomas Gerard. The Development and Evaluation of a
   Series of Recordings for Teaching Certain Critical Listening Abilities. Doctoral dissertation, Boston University, 1961. DS

Edgar, Kenneth Frank. The Validation of Four Methods of Improving Listening Ability. Doctoral dissertation,
   University of Pittsburgh, 1961.

Montgomery, Robert L. Listening Made Easy. New York: AMACOM,
   A Division of American Management Association, 1981.

Smeltzer, Larry R., and John L. Waltman. Managerial Communication: A Strategic Approach. New York: John Wiley &
   Sons, 1984.

1"

Before beginning the report
formatting assignments, be
sure you have read the material
on page 84 and studied the
models on pages 85-86.

Report 17

Key in the report shown at the
right and on page 88. Enter the
copy line for line and page for
page as shown, making the
corrections as indicated. You,
not the computer, are responsible for centering headings and
for spacing the report parts
properly.

When you have finished the
two pages, properly corrected,
proceed to page 89 and key in
the reference page and the title
page.

(Learning to Listen) *all caps*

Elementary
Grade school children are estimated to spend over half of

their school day listening. Managers in business spend up to 70

percent of their *workday* day listening. People, in general, usually spend

over 40 percent of their wa/king time listening. In spite of our

obvious dependence upon listening, few people listen well.

Listening and hearing *and* are two different but interrelated

processes. hearing is a mechanical activity that is difficult

to avoid; listening is a physical and#mental process that takes

deliberate effort {Smeltzer and Waltman, 1984, 188}. In simple

terms
words, you hear with your ears, but you listen with your brain.

Formal
Attempts to impro/ve listening skils *l* have been *ed* increasing since

World War II. These attempts fall into *two* too categories: self-

help strategies and directed-training programs.

Self-Help Strategies

Special books and parts of general communication books have

been written on how to listen *e* affectively. Such materials offer

better
a good understanding of the listening process and give guides

to help us practice better listening methods. For example, they

must
say that we should be highly motivated to listen *well*; that is, we

must intend to listen and not merely to hear. They tell us that

is saying
we must concentrate on what the speaker says and try to ignore

irrelevant distractions. They suggest what to listen for: the

main idea, major supporting points, and the message structure.

They urge us to mentally organize what is being said and to take notes in outline form. In other words, they tell us how to use the 75% difference in time between the speed of thinking and the slower speed of speaking.

The guides have been helpful to some individuals, but they have not been tested in a formal way to measure actual gains in listening effectiveness. Further, only a small percentage of people have the self-discipline and perseverance to profit from self-help strategies.

Directed-Training Programs

During the 1960's, several research studies were conducted to determine the effects of a variety of formal training methods on listening ability (for example, Devine, 1961; Edgar, 1961). Using a test-train-retest strategy, such researchers discovered that formal training programs with improvement goals established by a pretest and measured by a posttest provided the motivation to improve listening skills. They found also that specially designed training materials presented according to a prescribed schedule result in significant gains in listening effectiveness when compared with Listening Test Results from students who did not undergo the special training.

This is not to say that the guides offered by the self-help strategists do not work, for many of the suggestions were incorporated in the training programs. Rather, it says that if the guides are to work, they must be formally structured, practiced, and tested rather than attempted on a self-help basis.

2

Reference List

Process a reference list for the report using the information shown on index cards at the right. Key the copy line for line. Be sure to put the entries in alphabetical order. Remember to place the heading REFERENCES on line 12 from the top edge of the paper. Use SS mode; DS between the entries.

Proofread and correct (if necessary) the copy on the screen. Then key in the title page as directed below.

Title Page

Enter the information for a title page. Remember to begin the title on line 18.

Check the accuracy of your copy on screen; then store the report on your data disk as REP17. Print out a copy of the entire report.

Finally, assemble all pages of the report and staple them at three equally spaced points across the top edge (about a half inch from the top edge).

Devine, Thomas Gerard. *The Development and Evaluation of a Series of Recordings for Teaching Certain Critical Listening Abilities*. Doctoral dissertation, Boston University, 1961.

Montgomery, Robert L. *Listening Made Easy*. New York: AMACOM, A Division of American Management Association, 1981.

Edgar, Kenneth Frank. *The Validation of Four Methods of Improving Listening Ability*. Doctoral dissertation, University of Pittsburgh, 1961.

Smeltzer, Larry R., and John L. Waltman. *Managerial Communication: A Strategic Approach*. New York: John Wiley & Sons, 1984.

WORK EVALUATION

Answer the questions at the right. If any answer is no, make the needed corrections, print out a revised copy, and reassemble the report.

Self-Check Questions

	Yes	No
1. Did you place the report title on line 12 from top of page?	—	—
2. Did you leave 3 blank line spaces between the title and the first line of the body?	—	—
3. Did you use DS mode for the body of the report?	—	—
4. Did you DS above and below the side headings?	—	—
5. Are left and right margins approximately equal in width?	—	—
6. Did you leave a bottom margin of at least 1 inch on each page (exclusive of page number)?	—	—
7. Did you begin pages 2 and 3 of the report on line 10?	—	—
8. Did you center the page number on page 2 on line 62 from top of page?	—	—

	Yes	No
9. Did you enter the heading of the reference list on line 12?	—	—
10. Did you SS the items of the reference list?	—	—
11. Did you DS between the entries of the reference list?	—	—
12. Did you begin each reference list entry at the left margin and indent the other lines 5 spaces?	—	—
13. On the title page, did you enter the title on line 18?	—	—
14. Did you enter your name on line 34?	—	—
15. Did you DS between your name and the name of your school?	—	—
16. Did you enter the current date on line 52?	—	—

Key in the report shown at the right and on page 91. Enter the copy line for line and page for page as shown. You, not the computer, are responsible for centering headings and for spacing the report parts properly.

When you have finished the two pages, properly corrected, proceed to page 92 and key in the reference page and the title page.

OFFICE SUPPORT OCCUPATIONS OUTLOOK

Office support personnel, also called clerical workers, now are the largest occupational group in the nation. Their numbers are sure to grow at a rapid pace until at least the mid-1990's (Occupational Outlook Handbook, 1984, 202). Well-known job titles—Secretary, Stenographer, Typist, and Typewriting-Machine Operator head the list of office support needs (Dictionary of Occupational Titles, 1977, 153-154). All of these job classifications require high levels of keyboarding skill.

Secretaries and Stenographers

Secretaries perform widely varied administrative and clerical duties so that their employers can perform more difficult tasks. Their duties include scheduling appointments, organizing and maintaining files, filling out forms, giving information to callers, and typing. They also take and transcribe dictation.

Stenographers, on the other hand, have as their primary responsibility the taking and transcribing of dictation. They may also prepare a variety of other documents on the typewriter or a typewriter-like keyboard terminal, file, answer the telephone, and operate other office machines.

Jobs for secretaries are expected to increase faster than the average of all occupations in the immediate future. Office automation is not expected to diminish the need for secretaries, but it is already reducing the routine aspects of their work and increasing the value of their job role (Popham et al., 1983, 3).

Jobs for stenographers, however, are expected to continue the decline of recent years. Growing use of dictation machines has reduced the need for stenographers severely, and the "steno pool" is being replaced by the word processing center where most of the source documents come to keyboard operators on dictation disks, as handwritten copy, and as typewritten rough draft.

Typists and Typewriting-Machine Operators

This growing job class includes occupations "concerned primarily with recording, transcribing, transmitting, duplicating and receiving data by means of a typewriter or a machine with a typewriter-like keyboard" (D.O.T., 1977, 154). The numbers of such personnel are expected to grow about as fast as the average for all occupations throughout the 1980's.

Summary

Jobs in the office support group are projected to increase more than in any other job class except "other service workers" in the years ahead. Keyboarding skills, language skills, and computation skills are the keys to success in the technological / information age. As increasing automation reduces the number of routine tasks done by workers, clerical personnel should prepare themselves to move up in the organization or to move out.

2

Report 18, continued

Reference List

Process a reference list for the report using the information shown on index cards at the right. Key the copy line for line. Be sure to put the entries in alphabetical order. Use SS mode; DS between the entries.

Proofread and correct (if necessary) the copy on the screen. Then key in the title page as directed below.

Occupational Outlook Handbook. 1984-85 ed. Washington, DC: U. S. Government Printing Office, 1984.

Dictionary of Occupational Titles. 4th ed. Washington, DC: U. S. Government Printing Office, 1977.

Popham, Estelle, Rita Tilton, Howard Jackson, and Marshall Hanna. *Secretarial Procedures and Administration*. 8th ed. Cincinnati: South-Western Publishing Co., 1983.

Title Page

Enter the information for a title page.

Check the accuracy of your copy on screen; then store the report on your data disk as REP18. Print out a copy of the entire report.

Finally, assemble all pages of the report and staple them at three equally spaced points across the top edge (about a half inch from the top edge).

WORK EVALUATION

Answer the questions at the right. If any answer is no, make the needed corrections, print out a revised copy, and reassemble the report.

Self-Check Questions

	Yes	No
1. Did you place the report title on line 12 from top of page?	—	—
2. Did you DS above and below the side headings?	—	—
3. Are words properly divided at line endings?	—	—
4. Did you begin page 2 of the report on line 10?	—	—

	Yes	No
5. Did you center the page number on page 2 on line 62 from top of page?	—	—
6. Did you enter the heading of the reference list on line 12?	—	—
7. Are all book titles in the reference list underlined?	—	—
8. On the title page, did you enter the title on line 18?	—	—

PART 2
WORD PROCESSOR SIMULATION: TOPBOUND REPORTS

Key Reports 19 and 20 in topbound style, using the word processor simulation. Using Disk 2, follow the same procedures as for completing an unbound report (see pages 41-42), except for the following Print Settings:

Left margin:	10
Right margin:	77
Top line:	10
Page length:	60
Line spacing:	2
Page numbers:	B

Before beginning the report formatting assignments, study the material on page 93, which provides the procedures for using your computer as a word processor.

Report 19

Key in the report shown at the right and on page 95. The report is presented in script and corrected script form. Make the corrections indicated. Enter the copy continuously rather than line for line; the "word wrap" feature of the word processor will determine the line endings when the report is printed.

When you have finished the two pages, make needed corrections. Then proceed to page 96 and key in the reference page and the title page.

ERGONOMICS IN THE OFFICE

In factories and offices of the past, workers had to adapt to the machines and furniture they were given to use. In the early part of this century, time-and-motion study experts such as Frank and Lillian Gilbreth began looking for ways to improve work efficiency by creating a better relationship between people and the methods and machines they used to do work. In recent years, human factors engineers have been studying the effects of working conditions on the workers. According to Boone and Kurtz (1981, 440), "Human factors engineering applies information about human characteristics and behavior to the design of things people use, how they are used, and the environment in which people live and work." In the office environment, human factors engineering goes under the name "ergonomics."

"Ergonomics is the study of ways to make work less taxing physiologically" (Bedeian and Glueck, 1983, 306). Dictionaries define it as "the science that seeks to adapt work or working conditions to suit the worker." In our emerging high-tech information era, increasing attention is being given and must continue to be given to the reported adverse effects of high-tech factors in the workplace on human workers. These effects are both physiological and psychological in nature and are referred to as the high-touch factors of the office environment--ergonomics (Naisbitt, 1982, 35).

Office Lighting

From dimly lighted offices through intensely lighted offices of the past ~~bygone days~~, ergonomics has moved toward a very scientifically placed mix of lighting: ambient lighting and task lighting.

Task Lighting. Task lighting is ~~appropriately of~~ higher intensity than ambient lighting and is directed specifically to those areas where job tasks requiring high-intensity light are being performed. By using frosty bulbs or fluorescent tubes, even task lighting today, as compared to task lighting of the past, is relatively glarefree and results in less eyestrain, tension, and fatigue.

Office Furniture and Equipment

Ergonomically designed furniture and equipment is often adjustable so that it can be fitted to the individual who uses it. More and more office furniture is adjustable in height. VDT ~~Video~~ screens are often adjustable for light intensity and for correct viewing angle. Even some ~~such~~ keyboards have adjustable incline angles, according to Quible (1984, 161): "Office furniture that is ergonomically designed is more comfortable, less fatiguing ~~tiring~~, less mentally exhausting, and provides better support for the human body."

2

Ambient lighting. Ambient lighting, which is often trained on ceilings and walls and reflected downward, provides a very soft light in all areas where close task work is not performed -- aisles, hallways, and sitting areas. Such lighting is glareless and relaxing.

REVISIONS

BEFORE YOU PRINT A COPY OF THE REPORT, make the following revision:

Insert the ¶ about ambient lighting (given at the right) before the ¶ about task lighting. Then proceed to page 96, key in the reference page and title page, and print out a copy of the report.

Report 19, continued

Reference List

Enter the list of references line for line as shown at the right. Use SS mode; DS between entries.

When you finish entering the data, make any necessary corrections, then key in the title page as directed below.

Title Page

Prepare a title page: report title, your name and your school name; current date.

Make needed corrections, then store the report on your data disk as REP19. Print out a copy of the entire report. Assemble all pages of the report; staple the pages together across the top.

REFERENCES

Bedeian, Arthur G., and William F. Glueck. _Management._ 3d ed. Chicago: The Dryden Press, 1983.

Boone, L. E., and D. L. Kurtz. _Principles of Management._ New York: Random House, 1981.

"Ergonomics in the Office." _On Line Data Access._ August 1984, 20-23.

Naisbitt, John. _Megatrends: Ten New Directions Transforming Our Lives._ New York: Warner Books, 1982.

Quible, Zane K. _Administrative Office Management._ 3d ed. Reston, VA: Reston Publishing Company, Inc., 1981.

WORK EVALUATION

Answer the questions at the right. If any answer is no, make the needed corrections, print out a revised copy, and reassemble the report.

Self-Check Questions

Yes No

1. Did you place the report title on line 12 from top of page? ___ ___
2. Did you leave 3 blank line spaces between the title and the first line of the body? ___ ___
3. Did you use DS mode for the body of the report? ___ ___
4. Did you DS above and below the side headings? ___ ___
5. Did you leave a bottom margin of at least 1 inch on each page (exclusive of page number)? ___ ___
6. Did you begin page 2 of the report on line 10? ___ ___
7. Are left and right margins approximately equal in width? ___ ___

Yes No

8. Did you center the page number on page 2 on line 62 from top of page? ___ ___
9. Did you enter the heading of the reference list on line 12? ___ ___
10. Did you SS the items of the reference list? ___ ___
11. Did you DS between the entries of the reference list? ___ ___
12. Did you begin each reference list entry at the left margin and indent the other lines 5 spaces? ___ ___
13. On the title page, did you enter the title on line 18? ___ ___
14. Did you identify and correct all errors before printing out a copy of the report? ___ ___

Report 20

Key in the report shown at the right and on pages 98-99. The report is presented in rough-draft form, so make the corrections indicated. Enter the copy continuously rather than line for line.

When you have finished the three pages and corrected any errors you found, proceed to page 100 and key in the reference page and the title page.

YOUR JOB INTERVIEWS

Applying for a job is a lot of ~~hard~~ work. Organizing personnel*al*, education*al* and previous work information into a well-organized data sheet requires much thought and effort. Finding *a* job lead*s* and following ~~it~~ *them* up takes initiative and tenacity. *Preparing* ~~Writing~~ a letter to apply for a specific job requires not only good writing skills but also the ability to *select* ~~choose~~ specific items from the Data Sheet and organize them into a clear message that will convince the ~~employer~~ *reader* that your abilit*i*es and skills fit the job requirements. Yet all this effort does not land the job; it merely provides ~~for~~ the possibility that you will be called for an interview. The job interview is the critical test of whether the ~~desired~~ job becomes yours or someone else's.

The Interview--Behind the Scene

Learn about the company. If you get an interview, you know that the company has some interest at least in you as a potential employee. Your purpose during the interview, ~~is~~ therefore, is to increase that interest. To do so, you need to relate yourself to the firm, its products or services, and the *specific* ~~particular~~ type of job for which you are applying. This means *that* you must learn as much as you possibly can about the company, its personnel {particularly the interviewer and the person who would supervise your work}, and the primary features of tne job. The more you learn, the better you will be able to relate to the *pro*spective workplace.

Module C, Part 2 / Student-Formatted Topbound Report 20 (Word Processor Simulation)   **97**

Practice Dressing for the Interview. Like it or not, the way we look and behave determine how we are perceived by those we meet for the first time. "Clean, neat, and relaxed" are the words to keep in mind: freshly shampooed, neatly styled hair; clean hands and nails; clean, freshly pressed clothing; shined shoes. Dress for neither a party nor a picnic. It is better to dress "up" than to dress "down," but do not go too far either way. Dress and grooming should help you, not your plumage, show through.

If you habitually wear casual or leisure clothes and feel a bit stiff and uncomfortable when "dressed up," choose what you will wear to the interview and dress rehearse with a friend, with a family member, or in front of a mirror how you walk into a room; how you greet someone and shake hands; how you sit down; how you maintain your posture once seated; how you take leave of a person with whom you have been talking. Identify points when you appear stiff, awkward, or ill at ease. Work to eliminate these evidences of tension or stress through practice.

Practice answering questions that might be asked. If you anticipate questions that are likely to be asked in an interview and prepare answers to them, you will feel much more relaxed in the actual interview. A good list of typical questions is given in Wilkes and Crosswait {1981, 26-27} and in Gaither, Farr, and Pickrell {1983, 74-88}. You will be able to list others from your study of the company and the job for which you are applying.

As part of your rehearsal of the interview, have someone ask you questions from your list and evaluate your responses.

2

The Interview--Face to Face

Enter the interview area with a confident stride and erect posture. You maybe introduced to the interviewer, or you may be left on you're own. If the latter, simply proffer your hand for a handshake and then say: "Mr. Walton, I am Susan Porter. Thank you for inviting me to chat with you." Usually you will be asked to take a seat. If after a few moments you are not offered a seat, you may ask, "May I sit down, please?"

The interviewer usually will lead most of the initial conversation. If that does not happen after a moment or two following the introduction, be prepared to start the conversation with some bit of information you have learned about the company that has some relevance to your interest in the job that is available.

During the dialogue, try not to smoke even if you are offered the oportunity; do not slouch in the chair; do not place your purse or brief case on the interviewer's desk; do not let your eyes inspect things on the desk {Fregly, 1980, 356-360}.

Maintain eye contact with the interviewer. Answer questions thoughtfully, honesly, and directly. If some question is relevant to one of your strengths, embellish your answer with additional information. If a question plays to one your your weaknesses, answer as positively as you honestly can; but do not dwell on the point beyond what is essential. In always possible, try to help the interviewer to see that the abilities, skills, and attitudes you can bring to the job are more than the other applicants may possess. When the interview ends, leave with thanks and quiet dispatch.

3

REVISIONS
After you have printed the report, print out another copy of the report omitting the topic "Practice Dressing for the Interview."

Report 20, continued

Reference List

Enter the list of references line for line as shown at the right. Make the corrections as indicated. Use SS mode; DS between entries.

When all errors have been corrected, key in the title page.

Title Page

Prepare a title page for the report. Correct any errors, then store the report on your data disk as REP20. Print out a copy of the entire report.

Assemble all pages and staple them together across the top.

REFERENCES _Leave 3 blank line spaces._

Blackledge, Walter L. and Ethel H. Blackledge. The Job You Want--How to Get it. 3d ed. Cincinnati: South-Western Publishing Co., 1983.

Farr, J. Michael, Richard Gaither, and R. Michael Pickrell. The Work Book--Getting the Job You Want. Bloomington, IL: McKnight Publishing Company, 1983.

Fregly, Bert. Help Wanted: Everything You Need to Know to Get the Job You Deserve. Palm Springs, CA: ETC Publications, 1980.

Kughner, John A. How to Find and Apply for a Job. 4th ed. Cincinnati: South-Western Publishing Co., 1982.

Wilkes, Mary, and Bruce Crosswait. Professional Development: The Dynamics of Success. New York: Harcourt Brace Jovanovich, Inc., 1981.

WORK EVALUATION

Answer the questions at the right. If any answer is no, make the needed corrections, print out a revised copy, and reassemble the report.

Self-Check Questions

	Yes	No
1. Did you place the report title on line 12 from top of page?	—	—
2. Did you DS above and below the side headings?	—	—
3. Did you underline paragraph headings and end them with a period?	—	—
4. Did you leave a bottom margin of at least 1 inch on each page (exclusive of page number)?		
5. Did you begin pages 2 and 3 of the report on line 10?	—	—

	Yes	No
6. Did you center the page number on pages 2 and 3 on line 62 from top of page?	—	—
7. Did you enter the heading of the reference list on line 12?	—	—
8. Did you begin each reference list entry at the left margin and indent the other lines 5 spaces?	—	—
9. Did you underline all book titles in the reference list?	—	—
10. On the title page, did you enter the title on line 18?		

Sources of Additional Report-Formatting Activities

After you have learned the basic procedures for formatting reports, you may want to improve your skills by formatting reports from other sources using the Word Processor simulation or the Typewriter simulation option on the Report Formatting disks. Additional reports, from two South-Western Publishing keyboarding/typewriting texts, are listed below. Each of these reports has been checked to be sure that it can be acceptably formatted using the "word wrap" feature of the Word Processor simulation. Other reports could be formatted using the Report Formatting disks, but some of them will result in rather ragged right-hand margins.

For additional practice, select a report from the appropriate textbook below. Sign on to the computer using Report Formatting Disk 1 for an unbound report and Report Formatting Disk 2 for a leftbound or topbound report. At the Main Menu choose which simulation you wish to use (Word Processor or Typewriter). Follow the formatting guides provided in *Report Formatting* (even if they differ from the text you are using). When you save a report, give it a name of up to eight characters (spaces are not allowed). Use that name whenever you want to retrieve the report to view, edit, or print it.

College Keyboarding/Typewriting, 11th Edition (Complete Course)

UNBOUND REPORTS

53c, p. 98
54d, p. 100
74c, p. 137
136c, p. 249
140b, p. 253
150b Problem 1, p. 270
152d Job 2, p. 276
163b-168b Job 4, p. 294
171b-176b Job 11, p. 312
186c Job 2, p. 331
225c Job 2, p. 396

LEFTBOUND REPORTS

137b Problems 1 & 2, p. 251
152d Job 1, p. 276
163b-168b Job 3, p. 294
163b-168b Job 7, p. 296
186c Job 1, p. 331

TOPBOUND REPORTS

225c Job 3, p. 396

College Keyboarding/Typewriting, 11th Edition (Intensive Course)

UNBOUND REPORTS

39c Problem 1, p. 81
40c, p. 82
49c, p. 102
91c, p. 192
93b Problem 1, p. 195
100b Problem 1, p. 211
108b-110b Job 4, p. 229
113b-117b Job 9, p. 243
123c Job 2, p. 257
150b Job 2, p. 308

LEFTBOUND REPORTS

108b-110b Job 3, p. 229
123c Job 1, p. 257

TOPBOUND REPORTS

150b Job 3, p. 308

CREATING YOUR OWN REPORTS

You can use the typewriter and word processor simulations to key your own reports. Decide which style report you want to use and follow the procedures for using the simulation with that style report. When you save your report, give it a name of up to eight characters (spaces are not allowed). Use that name whenever you want to retrieve the report to view, edit, or print it.

APPENDICES

APPENDIX A
FORMATTING OR INITIALIZING A DATA DISK

Each student using the MICROCOMPUTER KEYBOARD-ING/FORMATTING APPLICATIONS series should have a separate data disk for each Formatting set (Letters, Reports, Tables). To create a data disk, format or initialize a blank 5¼" disk by copying the Disk Operating System (DOS) for your brand of microcomputer onto it. Follow directions for the brand(s) of microcomputer(s) in use. Use only a soft-tipped pen to label the data disks.

Apple

(1) Insert a DOS 3.3 System Master disk into the drive (Drive 1 if the microcomputer has two drives); close the disk drive door.
(2) Turn on the microcomputer. (The Apple prompt—]—appears.)
(3) *One Disk Drive*—Remove the DOS 3.3 System Master disk; insert a blank disk into the drive and close the drive door.
   Two Disk Drives—Insert a blank disk into Drive 2.
(4) *One Disk Drive*—Key INIT HELLO, D1, then strike RETURN.
   Two Disk Drives—Key INIT HELLO, D2, then strike RETURN. (The red light on the drive door is on while a disk is formatted.)
(5) When the red light goes off, remove the disk(s) from the disk drive(s).
(6) Turn off the microcomputer.

To Make Additional Data Disks: After Step 4, remove the newly formatted disk from the disk drive and insert another blank disk. Repeat Step 4.

IBM PC

(1) Insert a PC-DOS System disk into the drive (Drive A if the microcomputer has two drives); close the disk drive latch.
(2) Turn on the microcomputer. (*Wait* until the flashing cursor appears, a "beep" is emitted, the red light on the drive door goes off, and the following prompt appears on the screen: Enter new date: ____.)
(3) Key the current date; strike ENTER (↵). (Or simply strike ENTER.) (The following prompt appears on the screen: Enter new time: ____.)
(4) Key the time; strike ENTER (↵). (Or simply strike ENTER.) (A copyright message with A>____ on the last line appears on the screen.)

(5) *One Disk Drive*—Key FORMAT A: then strike ENTER. (The following prompt appears on the screen: Insert new diskette for drive A: and strike any key when ready____.) Remove the PC-DOS System disk; insert a blank disk into the disk drive.
   Two Disk Drives—Key FORMAT B: then strike ENTER. (The following prompt appears on the screen: Insert new diskette for drive B: and strike any key when ready____.) Insert a blank disk into Drive B.
(6) Strike the space bar (or any key) to continue. ("Format complete" appears on the screen, followed by a prompt to format another data disk.)
(7) If you want to format another data disk, strike Y(es) and respond to the prompts on the screen. If you do not want to format another data disk, strike N(o).
(8) Remove the disk(s) from the drive(s).
(9) Turn off the microcomputer.

TRS-80 Model III and Model 4

(1) Turn on the microcomputer.
(2) *One Disk Drive*—Insert a TRSDOS 1.3 System Master disk into the drive; close the drive door.
   Two Disk Drives—Insert a TRSDOS 1.3 System Master disk into Drive 0. Insert a blank disk into Drive 1. Close the drive doors.
(3) Press the orange (reset) button on the microcomputer keyboard.
(4) When the "date" prompt appears on the screen, key the current date. Key the time (or simply strike ENTER) when the "time" prompt appears. ("TRSDOS Ready" appears on the screen.)
(5) Key BACKUP then strike ENTER.
(6) When SOURCE Drive Number? appears, key 0 and strike ENTER.
(7) *One Disk Drive*—When DESTINATION Drive Number? appears, key 0 and strike ENTER.
   Two Disk Drives—When DESTINATION Drive Number? appears, key 1 and strike ENTER.
(8) When SOURCE Disk Master Password? appears, key PASSWORD and strike ENTER.
(9) *One Disk Drive*—The copying process begins. You will be instructed to change disks several times during the process. Whenever Insert DESTINATION Diskette <ENTER> flashes, remove the TRSDOS 1.3 System Master disk, insert the blank disk, and

strike ENTER. Whenever Insert SOURCE Diskette <ENTER> flashes on the screen, remove the blank disk, insert the TRSDOS 1.3 System Master disk, and strike ENTER.

Two Disk Drives—The copying process takes place.

(10) "Backup Complete" appears when the copying process is complete. (The message 00 Flawed Tracks appears on the screen.)

(11) Remove the disk(s) from the drive(s).

(12) Turn off the microcomputer.

To Make Additional Data Disks:

One Disk Drive—After Step 10, remove the newly formatted disk from the disk drive and insert the TRSDOS 1.3 System Master disk. Repeat Steps 5-10.

Two Disk Drives—After Step 10, remove the newly formatted disk from the disk drive and insert another blank disk. Repeat Steps 5-10.

APPENDIX B   Summary of Commands for Computer-Formatted Exercises

Function	Apple	TRS-80	IBM
Backspace	←	←	←
Caps lock	Caps lock key	Shift-∅/ Caps lock key	Caps lock key
Carriage return	RETURN	ENTER	Enter Key (←)
Command summary	Control-Z	Control-Z	Control-Z
Erase	Control-E/ Delete key	Control-E	Control-E/ Delete key
Escape	ESC	CLEAR	ESC
Execute	Control-X	Control-X	Control-X
Margin release	Control-R	Control-R	Control-R
Quit (view document only)	Control-Q	Control-Q	Control-Q
Scroll document (view document only)	↑ ↓	↑ ↓	↑ ↓
Space	Space bar	Space bar	Space bar
Tab key	TAB	→	Tab key (⇆)
Underline	Control-L	Control-L	Control-L

APPENDIX C   Summary of Commands for Typewriter Simulation

Function	Apple	TRS-80	IBM
Access format screen	Control-F	Control-F	Control-F
Backspace	←	←	←
Caps lock	Caps lock key	Shift-∅/ Caps lock key	Caps lock key
Carriage return	RETURN	ENTER	Enter Key (←)
Command summary	Control-Z	Control-Z	Control-Z
Erase	Control-E/ Delete key	Control-E	Control-E/ Delete key
Margin release	Control-R	Control-R	Control-R
New page	Control-N	Control-N	Control-N
Quit	Control-Q	Control-Q	Control-Q
Space	Space bar	Space bar	Space bar
Tab clear	Control-C	Control-C	Control-C
Tab key	TAB	→	Tab key (⇆)
Tab purge	Control-P	Control-P	Control-P
Tab set	Control-S	Control-S	Control-S
Underline	Control-L	Control-L	Control-L
Upward scroll	↑	↑	↑

APPENDIX D Summary of Commands for Word Processor Simulation

Function	Apple	TRS-80	IBM
ENTRY MODE			
Cancel entry	ESC	CLEAR	ESC
Caps lock	Caps lock key	Shift-Ø/ Caps lock key	Caps lock key
Carriage return	RETURN	ENTER	Enter key (←⅃)
Center	Control-C	Control-C	Control-C
Embedded formatting codes			
Change margins	*L, *R	*L, *R	*L, *R
Change spacing	*S	*S	*S
Eject page	*E	*E	*E
Insert blank lines	*B	*B	*B
Suppress page numbers	*P	*P	*P
Erase	←	←	←
Execute	Control-X	Control-X	Control-X
Tab key	TAB	→	Tab key (⇆)
Tab line	Control-T	Control-T	Control-T
Tab clear	c	c	c
Tab execute	RETURN	ENTER	Enter key (←⅃)
Tab purge	p	p	p
Tab select	←→	←→	←→
Tab set	s	s	s
Underline	Control-L	Control-L	Control-L
CURSOR MOVEMENT MODE			
Cursor movement			
Beginning	Control-B	Control-B	Control-B/HOME
End	Control-E	Control-E	Control-E/END
Left/Right	←→	←→	←→
Up/Down	↑↓	↑↓	↑↓
Delete	Control-D	Control-D	Control-D/DELETE
Entry	Control-N	Control-N	Control-N/INSERT
Quit	Control-Q	Control-Q	Control-Q
DELETE MODE			
Cancel deletion	ESC	CLEAR	ESC
Delete text	Space bar	Space bar	Space bar
Execute	Control-X	Control-X	Control-X
Retrieve text	←	←	←

INDEX

CF = computer-formatted exercises
TW = typewriter simulation
WP = word processor simulation